MARY
in her own words
THE MOTHER OF GOD IN SCRIPTURE

FATHER GARY CASTER

FOREWORD BY ARCHBISHOP JOHN J. MYERS

SERVANT
BOOKS

PUBLISHED BY ST. ANTHONY MESSENGER PRESS
CINCINNATI, OHIO

Excerpts from *Story of a Soul,* translated by John Clarke, OCD, copyright ©1996 by
Washington Province of Discalced Carmelites, used by permission of ICS Publications
2131 Lincoln Road, N.E. Washington, DC 20002, USA, www.icspublications.org.

Excerpts from the English translation of the *Catechism of the Catholic Church (CCC)* for
the United States of America copyright © 1994, United States Catholic Conference, Inc.–
Libreria Editrice Vaticana. English translation of the *Catechism of the Catholic Church:
Modifications from the Editio Typica* copyright © 1997, United Staes Catholic Conference,
Inc., Libreria Editrice Vaticana. Used with permission.

Unless otherwise noted, Scripture passages have been taken from the *Revised Standard
Version,* Catholic edition. Copyright 1946, 1952, 1971 by the Division of Christian
Education of the National Council of the Churches of Christ in the USA. Used by
permission. All rights reserved. (Note: The editors of this volume have made minor
changes in capitalization to some of the Scripture quotations herein. Please consult the
original source for proper capitalization.)

Cover and book design by Mark Sullivan
Cover image: El Greco, Holy Family with Saint Anne, detail: Virgin Mary.
Photo credit: Erich Lessing/Art Resource, NY

LIBRARY OF CONGRESS CATALOGING-IN-PUBLICATION DATA

Caster, Gary, 1961-
  Mary, in her own words : the mother of God in Scripture / Gary Caster.
     p. cm.
  ISBN-13: 978-0-86716-790-0 (pbk. : alk. paper)
  ISBN-10: 0-86716-790-4 (pbk. : alk. paper) 1. Mary, Blessed Virgin, Saint–Biblical
teaching. I. Title.

BT611.C37 2006
232.91–dc22

                                        2006020324

ISBN-13: 978-0-86716-790-0
ISBN-10: 0-86716-790-4

Published by Servant Books, an imprint of
St. Anthony Messenger Press
28 W. Liberty St.
Cincinnati, OH 45202
www.ServantBooks.org

Printed in the United States of America

Printed on acid-free paper

  07 08 09 10 5 4 3 2

For Raquel, my sister
Requiescat in pace.

CONTENTS

THE GOSPEL OF JESUS CHRIST HAS BEEN ENTRUSTED TO THE church, which has proclaimed that saving Word and celebrated the salvation it offers from generation to generation. For those who hear and embrace that Word, it is not enough that it remain external. The Word has to reach and transform our very hearts. Allowing God's grace to create an internal response, a personal relationship, with Jesus and through him with God the Father and God the Holy Spirit, is an integral aspect of discipleship.

This intimate relationship is not restricted to God alone; it extends to all our sisters and brothers in the faith and in a particular way to those who have reached our common goal of heaven. We are in communion with one another.

The church recognizes the unique role of the Blessed Virgin Mary. From Holy Scripture we learn of her singular relationship with Jesus and his disciples. Her motherhood has enriched the lives of the faithful over the centuries.

Father Gary Caster, understanding the importance of the interior life for the believer, has produced a beautiful and fruitful reflection on the Blessed Virgin Mary, drawing from her very words preserved in the New Testament. His work will enable many to deepen their relationship with God by attending and responding to the words and actions of the first and greatest disciple of the Lord Jesus.

I pray that those who read this book may experience a powerful and maternal transformation as the Blessed Mother leads them ever closer to Jesus, her son, our Savior and Lord.

–Most Revered John J. Myers
Archbishop of Newark, New Jersey

NEITHER AS A PRIEST NOR AS A CHRISTIAN WOULD ANYONE confuse me with Saint Louis de Montfort or Saint Maximilian Kolbe. I'm simply a man who has been captivated by the mother of the Savior since my childhood. What initially fascinated me and continues to do so was her willingness to appear to children. In fact, when I was nine years old I spent the entire summer expecting her to appear to me, just as she had to the three young peasants of Fatima. I was convinced Mary would come to me, open the earth and show me hell. It was a long summer; she never came.

From about the fourth grade on I began to read whatever I could find about the mother of Jesus. Each spiritual work and all the stories of apparitions—those approved and those unapproved—continued to draw me closer to her.

I learned to pray the rosary, something I continue to do almost daily. I have no trouble losing myself in its rhythm, its language and its mysteries. As soon as I make the Sign of the Cross and begin running the beads through my fingers, I fall away from all else and drift within the wonder of God's plan of redemption. Yet I must confess that I am extremely uncomfortable praying the rosary with others, something my younger sister always encouraged me to "get over."

Similarly, my relationship with Mary is private and deeply personal. As a priest I understand the importance of authentic devotion to Mary, but I nonetheless shy away from speaking openly with others about how Mary's love sustains and comforts me. While I have encouraged others to draw close to her, I have refrained from sharing what's in my heart concerning this beautiful woman who has been so misunderstood and, at times, so cavalierly maligned.

The following reflections on her words in Scripture are an attempt to overcome this reluctance. Perhaps revealing the thoughts of my heart (see Luke 2:35) will be a means by which others may open their hearts to Mary.

FROM THE EARLIEST DAYS OF CHRISTIANITY THE CHURCH HAS held up certain Christian men and women as examples of what it means to love and serve the Lord. The heroic witness and passionate love of the saints have inspired countless generations. The records of their lives and of their words have become rules of faith for those who seek to understand better the mysteries of God and the love expressed in the Person of his Son.

The saints show us Christ from the unique perspectives of their concrete historical circumstances and encourage us to embrace and express Christ's love from within our own. We are called not so much to imitate their ways of life as to do what they did: fall passionately in love with Jesus.

This "great...cloud of witnesses," as Hebrews 12 describes the saints in glory, has an impressive roster of men and women of all ages and from every state of life. It is safe to say that there is someone for everyone, and the church encourages her members to find at least one saint whose life story resonates with their own. This spiritual friendship can become the means by which a greater understanding and deeper experience of God's love floods and enriches one's life.

The saints are more than Christian role models; they are our truest Christian friends. Our communion with them is a gift that Christ extends to us, a gift of tremendous value for those who choose to accept it. Through a relationship with a "heavenly friend," we open ourselves not only to Christ but also to the other members of the heavenly coterie. The saints introduce us to other saints, so our heavenly friendships continually increase. This mutual and reciprocal communion of love is a great work of the Spirit of the living God.

Jesus, the one mediator between God and man, is the means by which we have real friendships with those "who have gone before us marked with the sign of faith."[1] Our communion with the great cloud of witnesses expands as they draw us into deeper union with the One who gave shape and direction to their lives on earth. We can trust that the holy men and women with whom we find friendship will help us on our pilgrim journey.

Mary's Little Flower

One young woman whose life continues to speak to the hearts of men and women throughout the world is Saint Thérèse of the Child Jesus, or Thérèse of Lisieux. Pope Saint Pius X called her "the greatest saint of modern times."[2] She served as a personal inspiration to other men and women, such as Maximilian Kolbe and Mother Teresa of Calcutta, whom the church would later proclaim to be in her company. She has been my close personal friend for almost forty years. I have found her to be a great companion in coming to know not only the Lord but also his mother.

Saint Thérèse of Lisieux loved the Blessed Mother. In fact, Our Lady was such an important figure in Thérèse's spiritual life that one could argue that her spiritual doctrine, "the little way of spiritual childhood," is patterned after

Mary's life. Indeed, I think of Mary as "the mother of the little way."

I find that reading the autobiography of Saint Thérèse, *The Story of a Soul,* is like reading a subtle treatise on Mary. Although Jesus is at the center of her story, Thérèse seems to take for granted Mary's important role in the lives of believers. Devotion to Mary is not just a footnote in the saint's life. Thérèse is a daughter of Mount Carmel, and Our Lady punctuates the whole of her life.

Those who are familiar with the life of Saint Thérèse know about the miraculous cure she and her family attributed to Mary. The illness and the cure came at a pivotal time in the saint's life. Thérèse was nine years old. Her sister Pauline had entered the Carmelite convent of Lisieux, and her sister Marie was intent on doing the same. Thérèse was losing the two women who had stepped in to take the place of her mother, who had died five years earlier. In the midst of this emotionally difficult situation, Thérèse became seriously ill.

Thérèse's family arranged for a novena of Masses to be said for her healing at the Church of Our Lady of Victories in Paris. On the Sunday during this novena, her three sisters gathered around her bed and prayed before a statue of Mary "with the fervor of a mother begging for the life of her child." Thérèse prayed too, and "All of a sudden the Blessed Virgin appeared *beautiful* to me, so *beautiful* that I had never seen anything so attractive....what penetrated to the very depths of my soul was the *'ravishing smile of the Blessed Virgin.'*"[3]

Thérèse's pain was relieved immediately, but she was reluctant to talk about this event. "Never will I tell anyone" was her first reaction, "for my *happiness would then disappear.*"[4]

The information she eventually did record makes it clear that Mary was to remain an important presence throughout the rest of her life.

> I put all my heart into *speaking* to her, into consecrating myself to her as a child throwing itself into the arms of its mother, asking her to watch over her. It seems to me the Blessed Virgin must have looked upon her little flower and *smiled* at her, for wasn't it she who cured her with a *visible smile?* Had she not placed in the heart of her little flower her Jesus, the Flower of the Fields and the Lily of the Valley?[5]

Mary's intervention was more than a physical healing; it opened Thérèse to a profound understanding of this remarkable woman whom the church refers to as the Mother of God, Our Lady of Victories, the Mother of the Church and the Mother of the Eucharist.

Although these titles of Mary are familiar to all who have a devotion to her, Thérèse used two of them in new and bold ways. Her insights give us a fresh way of thinking of and reflecting on the spoken words of Mary that have been preserved in sacred Scripture. A brief examination of just a few of the saint's insights will prove my point.

Mother of God

For Thérèse the motherhood of Mary remains firmly tied to what it naturally expresses: Mary's relationship with Jesus. And yet her motherhood means much more.

Thérèse grasps the term primarily from the perspective

of vocation. The Father called Mary not only to give birth to Jesus but also to live and express her maternity through her relationship with us. Mary's vocation demands that she give herself completely to us, responding to our needs on behalf of her son. Saint Thérèse knew that she had access to Mary's help as a member of the church. "If some disturbance overtakes me, some embarrassment," she wrote, "I turn very quickly to her and as the most tender of Mothers she always takes care of my interests."[6]

In order to understand this "most tender of Mothers," one must understand that Mary's experience of holiness was effected by God's invitation to her to become his Son's mother. Mary was certainly sinless by virtue of the privilege of her immaculate conception, but she didn't begin to understand this "fullness of grace" until she conceived the child Jesus in her womb. As her life with Jesus progressed and her vocation as his mother unfolded, Mary moved ever deeper into the mystery of her own salvation. In the context of her vocation as Jesus' mother she awakened to the significance of God's saving action in her life.

I see a similar action of God in the life of Thérèse. Through the waters of baptism God purified her of original sin and gave her a new life in grace. As a young girl God's love was already at work against the effects of concupiscence. Through her life of prayer and her receptivity to God's love, Thérèse's vocation became clear.

Just as Mary's life of grace was filled out and formed according to the unique vocation to which God had called her, so too was the life of Thérèse. After her entrance into Carmel she would understand in new and richer ways what it meant to live a grace-filled life. For example, she saw the blessings of the life of obedience: "What anxieties the Vow of Obedience frees us from! How happy are simple religious! Their only compass being their Superiors' will, they are always sure of being on the right road; they have nothing to fear...even when it seems that their Superiors are wrong."[7]

Thérèse regarded Mary as a woman who can understand the desires born of a heart purified by God, a woman who will always aid others in accepting their vocations and living them faithfully. "The Blessed Virgin...was helping me prepare the dress of my soul," she wrote of her approach to her profession as a Carmelite. "As soon as this dress was completed all the obstacles went away by themselves."[8]

Thérèse recognized Mary as a woman who knows intimately and personally the love and mercy of God. Mary is all merciful because she was conceived in mercy to bear the Font and Source of mercy. In light of this Thérèse never hesitated in approaching Mary for help in any circumstance. Mary is the perfect mother because the child she bears is the source of graced living for all who are baptized into his life.

Our Lady of Victories

The second title of Our Lady that had special significance for Saint Thérèse is Our Lady of Victories. Recall that it was at the Church of Our Lady of Victories in Paris that the novena was offered for her healing when she was nine years old. Perhaps this prompted the young saint's interest in this title of Mary.

"Our Lady of Victories" is most commonly associated with Mary's intercession in the Battle of Lepanto on October

7, 1571. Through her intercession a small papal fleet defeated the Ottoman navy. But Thérèse isn't thinking of such a battle when she uses the expression. To be sure, the title does underscore Mary's role in the ongoing spiritual battle between the offspring of Eve and the powers and principalities of darkness, but Thérèse is never content with giving attention to the devil. Our Lady is more than just the victor over the original choice of Eve; she is the champion of grace. She embodies in her flesh, in her life, in her very person, what it means to be victorious—not because of anything she did but because of what God has done for her.

The privilege of being born without sin was a gift from God, and this condition of her birth was a victory over evil in Mary's life and subsequently in our lives too. Mary's Magnificat is the greatest victory song ever sung. God the Almighty truly "has done great things" (Luke 1:49).

Mary is Our Lady of Victories because she accepted the way God chose to exalt her. God redeemed her beforehand with a view to Christ. The announcement of the archangel Gabriel is a radical confirmation of what God had already done. Mary was not exalted from her lowliness because she said yes to the angel; she was exalted at the moment of her conception. When Mary said yes, she was saying yes to what God had already accomplished in and for her and yes to what God wants to accomplish in and for us.

Thérèse used the title Our Lady of Victories, one so dear to her and her family, as a celebration of what she believed about God. He is the seat of mercy, the One whose eternal love reaches toward the human family in general and toward Thérèse in unique and specific ways. "God showed me the same mercy He showed to King Solomon," she wrote. "He has not willed that I have one single desire which is not fulfilled....Instead of doing me any harm, of making me vain, the gifts which God showered upon me (without my having asked for them) drew me to *Him*; and I saw that He alone was *unchangeable,* that He alone could fulfill my immense desires."[9]

Just as Mary came to understand the victory that was hers solely by God's action, so did Thérèse. It was God's action that enabled her to enter the convent at a young age, so her whole life in Carmel, her vocation, was an expression of victory. Thérèse could have confident recourse to Our Lady of Victories because she was experiencing in her life what Mary experienced in hers: the Almighty doing great things for her.

Thérèse found in Mary a woman who understood her gratitude for the good works that God had accomplished for her salvation. The confirmation of this is the fact that the statue of Mary "smiled" at Thérèse when she was healed of her infirmity at the age of nine. Mary showed herself to be a woman not of intimidating power but of love and warmth.

Mary always comes to us with a language we can understand. The language of victory is the language of loving God with the same love with which he first loved us. For Saint Thérèse, Mary is a most essential tool in the grammar of God's love and mercy, for she punctuates the whole of the saint's life. Thérèse learned that Mary's *fiat* opened her to the fullness of God's riches because it opened Mary to his Son, the Victor over sin and death.

Our Mother, Too

These two titles of Mary, Our Lady of Victories and Mother of God, are more than mere acknowledgments that Mary enjoys eternal beatitude. Her maternity and her victory extend to all the church. Vatican II stated: "Taken up to heaven she did not lay aside this saving office but by her manifold intercession continues to bring us the gifts of eternal salvation....Therefore the Blessed Virgin is invoked in the Church under the titles of Advocate, Helper, Benefactress, and Mediatrix."[10] The council fathers understood so well the proper place of Mary in our lives.

The autobiography of Saint Thérèse not only makes this clear; it also presents the truth that God, Mary and all the angels and saints are easily approachable. Thérèse learned this herself when visiting the tomb of Saint Cecilia in Rome. Prior to the trip Thérèse had no special devotion to Cecilia, but she left with "more than devotion...; it was the real *tenderness of a friend.*"[11] Cecilia became a "confidante" for Thérèse, just as Mary remained for her more a mother than a queen. After agonizing over her difficulty in saying the rosary by herself—"more difficult for me than the wearing of an instrument of penance"—she acknowledged, "I think that the Queen of heaven, since she is *my MOTHER,* must see my good will and she is satisfied with it."[12] Saint Thérèse wants everyone to have recourse to this humble servant of God, whose *fiat* makes it possible for us to receive the Son in the Holy Eucharist.

As Saint Thérèse shows us, all spiritual realities must be appreciated within the context of relationship. We can begin experiencing here and now what God wants for us in eternity: intimate, loving communion through, with and in the

Person of his Son. The word *heaven* describes a relationship that has already begun, one that is lived in communion with the entire church. Mary's relationship with Jesus enables her to support others in achieving this because she experiences it in a way that no one else can. Only Mary is the mother of Jesus.

Heaven is the act of letting go and falling into the bottomless pool of God's love. It is a continual opening of oneself to the relationship begun in the waters of baptism. "I have found my place in the Church," Thérèse wrote. *"In the heart of the Church, I shall be Love.* Thus I shall be everything, and thus my dream will be realized."[13]

The part Mary continues to play in God's plan to gather all people to himself is intimately bound with the life and saving action of her son. Mary is the greatest of all saints, and her life gives us insight into the heart and mind of the God who "so loved the world that he gave his only-begotten Son" as our redeemer (John 3:16). Thus the words we hear her speak in Scripture are worthy of our attention and meditation.

PART ONE
MOTHER OF GOD

In the sixth month the angel Gabriel...came to her and said, "Hail, full of grace, the Lord is with you!" But she was greatly troubled at the saying, and considered in her mind what sort of greeting this might be. And the angel said to her, "Do not be afraid, Mary, for you have found favor with God. And behold, you will conceive in your womb and bear a son, and you shall call his name Jesus.

> He will be great, and will be called the Son of the Most High;
>
> and the Lord God will give to him the throne of his father David,
>
> and he will reign over the house of Jacob for ever;
>
> and of his kingdom there will be no end."

And Mary said to the angel, "How can this be, since I have no husband?" And the angel said to her,

> "The Holy Spirit will come upon you,
>
> and the power of the Most High will overshadow you;
>
> therefore the child to be born will be called holy,
>
> the Son of God...."

And Mary said, "Behold, I am the handmaid of the Lord; let it be to me according to your word." (Luke 1:26, 28–35, 38)

IN AD 431 THE BISHOPS OF THE CHURCH HAD THE SINGULAR honor of reaffirming the truth of Christ's humanity and divinity. In order to suppress the spreading influence of a theological heresy, the bishops chose to clarify a doctrine that had been presented over one hundred years earlier: that Jesus is both God and man in one divine person. They affirmed "that the Word, uniting to himself in his person the flesh animated by a rational soul, became man."[1] The bishops hoped to dispel once and for all any confusion about who Jesus is.

The Council of Ephesus therefore went on to declare Mary to be *Theotokos*—that is, "Mother of God." It is the mind of the church, then, that Mary is only properly and correctly understood with relation to her son. All claims about her must be reconciled with that which the church holds to be definitively true of Jesus. The light of Christ illuminates the lives of all believers, and the church has consistently held that this is especially true of Mary. Whatever we say about her relates to the child to whom she gave flesh and blood.

Unfortunately, many Christians refuse to acknowledge the distinctive character of the relationship the church has always celebrated between the Mother of God and her son. Some reduce her role to one of function, like a sort of incubator for the divine. It is important that all Christians know that the church continues to celebrate Mary's life and honor her with titles because she is an essential character in the divine plan of salvation.

Perhaps no other title honoring Mary of Nazareth is as familiar yet controversial as "Mother of God." Although the initial proclamation by the bishops at the Council of Ephesus was greeted with great enthusiasm by the faithful, there are many Christians today who think the title gives Mary the kind of attention that rightly belongs to God. These may be surprised to learn that Mary herself seems to share their sense of amazement at the role she was asked to play in the drama of salvation.

Gabriel enters into the quiet simplicity of Mary's life with an urgency and excitement that do not allow for studied reflection. There is no mention of returning after a few days have passed, giving her a chance to consider carefully what's been said. Mary's "troubled" thoughts betray her solidarity with those who wonder at the place she occupies in God's plan.

MARY'S FIRST WORDS IN SCRIPTURE APPEAR TO ME TO BE more than a question about the practical implications of the angel's words. The question Mary asks the messenger of God, "How can this be, since I have no husband?" (Luke 1:34), reveals both an uncommon humility and a tremendous depth of spirit. In order to appreciate the richness of these words, I want to separate them into two parts. This chapter will focus on the first part of Mary's response, "How can this be?"

Here I find expression of Mary's interior disposition following Gabriel's greeting, "Hail, full of grace, the Lord is with you!" (Luke 1:26). Her words draw us back to the book of Genesis, specifically to the accounts of creation and original sin found in the second and third chapters. Mary speaks from the human side of the distance between the Author of all that exists and the persons created to share his life. She speaks not for herself alone but on behalf of the entire created order. With her question the "eager longing" of creation (see Romans 8:19) finds its voice: "How can this be?"

How is it possible that a child of Adam and Eve, a woman born into a world disordered by sin, could find favor with God? "Why would God," she seems to be saying, "the unbounded Other, reach across the radical divide that separates man from him? Why would he address himself to a finite, limited creature?"

Through Gabriel God makes the amazing announcement: "I want to be known. And this is who 'I Am': I am the one who has favored you and chosen you, the One who has given you life, the One who now humbles himself before you." This is a radical and almost incomprehensible message, one addressed to all mankind even as it is to Mary.

The archangel's greeting pierces the heart of the young virgin of Nazareth. Luke tells us that she "was greatly troubled at the saying, and considered in her mind what sort of greeting this might be" (Luke 1:29). These words imply that Mary is not aware of the unique privilege of her conception— or at least of its purpose. God intervened to free her from the stain of original sin in order to make her a fitting receptacle for his Son. Saint Luke gives no suggestion that Mary is expecting a messenger from God to announce the unfolding of his plan of salvation. Mary is shocked, and the angel needs to assure her, "Do not be afraid, Mary, for you have found favor with God" (Luke 1:30).

Mary has never considered herself to be greater than any of God's people. She knows well that God is the Father of the Israelites, and she knows well the history of her people. Yet nothing has prepared her for this amazing announcement that will culminate in the fulfillment of that history.

While Mary seems unaware of the fact and the reason of her immaculate conception, surely she has been living with its effects throughout her young life. Her difference certainly marked her perception of reality. Imagine always desiring the good in a world that too often rejects it, living the light of redemption in the midst of darkness. Surely she has a blessed existence but perhaps a lonely one also.

The words of the angel cause the sentiments, questions and full range of Mary's life experiences to come into the light. Gabriel illuminates every nuance of grace that has acted within Mary since the first moment of her existence. Everything she has thought about herself (and perhaps even questioned) but never spoken aloud is suddenly laid bare.

God's election of her, his presence in her life and the depth of his favor are now exposed to scrutiny and perhaps to ridicule. Mary's life and her intimate relationship with God are no longer hers alone.

Mary's words are more than an expression of wonder and surprise; they are also a plea. It is as if she is asking the archangel to tell her how she is to live under the weight of his words. Being "full of grace" is a burden Mary is not certain how to carry. God has favored her, but how does one live the truth of such a bold proclamation?

Saint Peter seems to acknowledge this dilemma when confronted by the figure of Christ and his call. The overwhelming and troubling reality of God's presence moves Peter to throw himself at the feet of Jesus and beg him to go away (see Luke 5:4–9). The naked fact of God's love for us is something we simply cannot bear on our own. Living in unconditional, unbounded, unfathomable love, "how can this be?" Who of us can bear the confrontation with God's love? For humans this does seem impossible. We think of God's words to Moses, "Man shall not see me and live" (Exodus 33:20).

Mary wants to know how she is to bear the weight of God's love. While she has no reason to doubt the truth of the angel's claim, she has reason to ask, "How can this be?"

The reasonableness of her question draws attention to the second account of creation in Genesis, chapter two. Standing before the goodness of all created reality, realizing everything has been given to him by God, Adam is nonetheless alone. The immensity of God's love confronts him in creation, yet Adam can find nothing in that creation that will complete him. There is nothing that he can "render to the LORD for all his bounty" to him (Psalm 116:12).

Adam wants to give the whole of himself to God as a fruitful response to God's generous love. Adam finds nothing in creation that will enable him to do so, nothing in creation that completes him. God's creative love is a burden Adam cannot carry by himself; he needs a suitable partner. God responds to Adam's loneliness and his desire to give himself in love—totally, faithfully, mutually and fruitfully to another. Only in giving and receiving love will Adam be able to respond to and give thanks for God's favor.

Mary's response to Gabriel seems to echo the alone-ness of the first man. Like Adam, she needs to find a suitable means for expressing her gratitude. She doesn't want to carry alone the burden of the angel's announcement. Mary wants to give herself in a way that is a total, faithful and fruitful response to God's loving favor. How can she possibly repay the Lord for his goodness to her?

The archangel Gabriel confirms that with God all things are indeed possible. God already has in mind the most fitting way for Mary to give herself in fruitful thankfulness for what the Almighty has done. God guarantees that Mary will never have to carry the weight of his loving favor alone. "How can this be?"

CHAPTER THREE
"I HAVE NO HUSBAND"

THE SECOND PART OF MARY'S QUESTION TO THE ARCHANGEL Gabriel arises from "the difference" that has favored her from the moment of her conception. Being immaculately conceived didn't put Mary at odds with others, but it made her different from them. This difference was something she surely must have felt. Therefore, "I have no husband" is more than a statement about her social standing or physical condition. While it most certainly encompasses these, it is at its core a theological statement.

Mary never could have found a "suitable partner" with whom she could give fruitful thanks to God's generous favor. Mary has no husband because, quite literally, there is no man to whom she could give herself totally, fruitfully, exclusively and physically. There is no man whose gift of self to her could be completely reciprocal. The disorder in human relationships caused by original sin would prevent any man from recognizing Mary as "bone of my bones and flesh of my flesh" (Genesis 2:23).

Mary's spiritual purity permeates her whole being. She therefore embodies the action of God; she bears his favor in her flesh. Her virginity is not merely a social, religious or moral choice, nor simply one aspect of her life. It is the ultimate truth of how she exists in the world. Mary may not know the reason behind it, but she nonetheless embraces her condition: "I have no husband," she says, though she is betrothed to Joseph.

Virginity is Mary's stance before the world, just as it is her stance before God. The completeness for which she longs is something that only God can satisfy. She can sing the words of Psalm 62 as her own, "For God alone my soul waits in silence....He only is my rock and my salvation" (Psalm 62:1, 2).

Revealing her virginity to the archangel is a bold declaration about her openness to God. There is no man who can participate in her complete openness to God, an openness of which her virginity is the concrete, physical sign, a kind of sacrament of God's creative possibilities. Mary's virginity is a statement that God makes to all of humanity of the single-hearted devotion to him that yields redemption and favor.

> Blessed are the people who know the festal shout,
>> who walk, O LORD, in the light of your countenance,
> who exult in your name all the day,
>> and extol your righteousness.
> For you are the glory of their strength;
>> by your favor our horn is exalted. (Psalm 89:15–17)

Mary has remained a virgin not to renounce human fruitfulness and sexual love but to affirm their original sacredness. God and Mary (the divine and the human) meet each other in the reality of her physical chasteness. Mary's virginity is the only place the Incarnation could be possible. Her immaculate state results from the direct action of God. Mary's decision to embrace the unique and not fully understood condition of her existence allows God and humanity to meet and, in fact, to become one. Virginity in Mary is God's openness to the world, even as it is Mary's openness to God.

Mary has already been living her life as a response to God, even though she does not know his plan. The simplicity of her response to Gabriel demonstrates the kind of trust with which she has embraced her life. She has chosen virginity as a personal expression of her total self-giving to God. Now she is troubled because the message of the angel seems to call into question the validity of the choice she's made.

Mary could not have absorbed the full impact of Gabriel's message were she not already spiritually recollected. She must have spent much time in prayerful reflection about how she could make her life an offering to God. If God does indeed have a plan for her—as unimaginable as the archangel's words may be—then first things first: "I have no husband."

Mary does not address directly the details of the announcement, such as the characterization of the child or the nature of his kingdom. She knows that if this is truly the will of God, then it will come to pass. Her entirely practical question shows that she understands the urgency with which Gabriel announces God's plan. Mary has her eyes focused on what she is capable of doing. In order to play her part in this, Mary makes it abundantly clear that she's going to need the help of God: "I have no husband."

Mary already seems moved toward giving her yes to Gabriel. If God has indeed chosen her, then there is for Mary only one possible response: to give in, to submit, to accept. Yet before she can fully and freely do so, she wants to be certain that the way she has chosen to respond receptively to God—her virginity—has been according to his will.

In the face of the archangel's announcement and her unlikely election, Mary remains irrevocably humble. She lays her life before Gabriel, placing before him her relationship with God and her intimate and deeply personal desire to offer him thanks and praise. Although Gabriel has already told her that she has found favor with God, Mary wants to be certain that she has in no way rejected God's favor or thwarted his plan. She does this simply by stating the truth of her condition: "I have no husband."

This encounter is unlike the numerous encounters between an angel and a human being that Scripture records. Yet Mary's response places her squarely within the company of those who, faced with God's favor and election, have sought angelic reassurance that their lives truly could be of service to God. She is a daughter of Abraham, Isaac and Jacob, and she has been faithful to God's covenant. If the way she has chosen to live her life for God within the community of his people has been correct, then the archangel will reassure her of this by the way he responds to what she has said.

CHAPTER FOUR
"Behold, I Am the Handmaid of the Lord"

God sends the archangel Gabriel to the Virgin of Nazareth. As a created spirit who serves as God's messenger, everything that Gabriel knows is particular to and ordered toward the messages he bears. The way in which Gabriel greets Mary reveals the depths of his knowledge of God's plan both for humanity and for the young woman to whom God has sent him.

And yet the archangel's encounter with Mary is an opportunity for them both. It is a real experience for Gabriel, not one that can be reduced to the knowledge infused by God. Mary is present to the message but also to the messenger. Her response to him gives definitive shape to the information God has shared with Gabriel concerning human redemption. It allows God's plan to have "personality."

Mary's words don't add details to fill the gaps in Gabriel's knowledge about God's plan. Rather, her words, her bearing and her spirituality allow Gabriel to understand the plan of God from a new perspective. God sent Gabriel to deliver his message to Mary, but Mary is also God's gift to Gabriel. As Mary tries to communicate her thoughts and feelings clearly and responsibly, her manner betrays a certain solidarity with the heavenly messenger.

All the created spirits who freely choose to serve God now have Mary as a fruit of their decision. Mary personifies

God's openness to all the faithful angels, just as she does God's openness to humanity.

Gabriel's sensitivity to this incredible woman is reflected in the way that he addresses her question, "How can this be?" He tells Mary, "The Holy Spirit will come upon you, / and the power of the Most High will overshadow you; / therefore the child to be born will be called holy, / the Son of God" (Luke 1:35).

The archangel speaks to the implications of Mary's carefully chosen reply to his announcement. Mary's complete baring of her soul strikes Gabriel with awe. He sees the depth of her love for God and the sincerity of her desire to give thanks and praise to him. Mary's total openness to God is reflected in her docility toward Gabriel, and this resonates with his own being. As a created spirit who has freely chosen to serve God, he too is open to the One who has created and now sustains his existence, to the One humbling himself before this woman.

Gabriel understands and empathizes with all that Mary's response implies. He is more than a divine functionary; he comes to her and addresses her as a friend of God and a friend to her. His words reflect the fact that he understands and appreciates Mary as a person. His response is, in fact, one of the most respectful and encouraging in all of Scripture. He reassures Mary that God has found acceptable the way she has chosen to live. Her virginity is, in fact, God's means of fulfilling his plan of redemption. Her virginity is positive; it is active and dynamic, not passive and sterile. It is the gateway through which the King of Glory will enter (see Psalm 24).

Gabriel knows that Mary's longing for God is going to be realized both physically and spiritually in her. The assurance that he gives speaks to the totality of how she has been created: as a unity of spirit and flesh. The Holy Spirit, already introduced here as Mary's advocate, is the guarantor of God's respect for how Mary has chosen to live her life for him. The same creative spirit who hovered over the waters at the Creation (see Genesis 1:2) will hover over Mary.

Gabriel encourages Mary to step into the creative power of God: "The Holy Spirit will come upon you, and the power of the Most High will overshadow you" (Luke 1:35). God's power does not violate, manipulate or dominate Mary; rather it affirms, enhances and participates in the decision Mary has made to give herself totally to God. Gabriel gives her news too of the pregnancy of Elizabeth, which is not only a part of the redemptive plan but also a sign of the creative initiative of God. With him "nothing will be impossible" (Luke 1:37).

Gabriel knows the full range of God's possibilities, and Mary embodies an opening to this potential. She who has longed to be complete in God senses through the archangel's message that her fulfillment is at hand. This exchange is one of more than mere words, for woman and archangel both come to know the God they serve in a deeper way.

Mary appears to accept the fact that this privileged exchange should end, lest it be too much for either of them to bear. I imagine her words escaping in almost a whisper. "Behold" is her invitation to Gabriel to look upon her as she is, to see her with the eyes of God. "See me for who I am," she seems to say, "a humble servant of the Most High."

Mary does not retreat from Gabriel; she exposes her new self-awareness: "I am the handmaid of the Lord." These are not words of passive acquiescence or resigned defeat; they are triumphant words, even if somewhat muted by the emotions flooding through their speaker. God has chosen to use the gift of her self in a creative way. Mary's love of God is genuinely fruitful.

The invitation Mary has received, the call, her vocation, is not simply something God wants her to do but something God wants her to be. She is to be the unique embodiment of God's possibilities, the unique expression of what God can accomplish. Mary begins to understand the nature of her difference. Any cloud of ignorance lifts, and she sees who she is: "the handmaid of the Lord" (Luke 1:38).

This recognition of identity in vocation is exciting, even as it is humbling and unimaginable. The archangel is telling Mary that she is the way in which the uncreated, infinite Other has chosen to limit and fix his communication with humanity. Mary's flesh will give flesh and blood to all that God longs to say to the human family. God is asking her to be wedded to his generative paternity in a unique and privileged way.

It isn't simply a womb that God needs but the totality of her being, including her personality. Like the words God spoke to Moses out of the burning bush, "I am the God of your father, the God of Abraham, the God of Isaac, and the God of Jacob" (Exodus 3:6), Mary's words are emphatically revelatory: "I am the handmaid of the Lord."

Mary is aware that the difference that has marked her life will now be more profound. But that is of little consequence in the light of knowing who she is and the person God created her to be. In the possibility of God, Mary provides the flesh and blood for the "in time and space" extension of God. Through, with and in her, God extends himself to humanity. God's extension toward us will have a name, Jesus. The child Mary will bear will truly be "Son of God."

Mary's life and the life of the child can never be separated. The child will be a real human being, related always and intimately to his mother. This relationship transcends the biological. The truth of the humanity of Jesus perfectly corresponds with the truth of his divinity. As the eternal Son, Jesus is the personal expression of the Father's self-giving love. As a man, Jesus incarnates the mutual giving of self between Mary and God the Father.

The life of Mary's child is wholly dependent upon her choice. God invites Mary to give voice to his personal word of love to humanity. Through her yes "the Word became flesh and dwelt among us, full of grace and truth." Through her yes "we have beheld his glory,...and from his fulness have we all received, grace upon grace" (John 1:14, 16). Through her yes "the life was made manifest, and we saw it" (1 John 1:2).

Mary's identity emerges from this radical encounter and this mysterious moment. As the Father's unique and perfect creation, Mary now knows herself and expresses herself in the divine light of this angelic visitation: "Behold, I am the handmaid of the Lord."

CHAPTER FIVE
"LET IT BE TO ME ACCORDING TO YOUR WORD"

NOW IT IS CLEAR: THERE IS NO TIME TO WASTE, NO CHANCE for second-guessing and endless, furtive speculation. The archangel Gabriel has addressed respectfully and clearly all that Mary finds troubling. She has only to accept or reject what the archangel has laid before her. There can be no question about the truthfulness of what has been revealed to her, for God cannot lie.

The total openness with which she has lived her life before God begs her to enter into the truth of God's plan. This is the moment for which she has lived her whole life; it is the moment God has had in mind for her since he spoke those initial creative words, "Let there be light" (Genesis 1:3).

Up to this point Mary has been completely transparent before the archangel, and in turn God, acting through Gabriel, has been completely transparent before Mary, the wonderful "work of his hands" (Job 34:19). Mary understands what her life is all about. God has accepted her total gift of self and is offering himself to her in return.

Now has salvation come in the humble freedom of the Almighty, who opens himself to the gentle humility of his own creation. "Here I am," God seems to be saying. "Do you want and will you welcome that which your soul has yearned for?" And Mary's freedom embraces the freedom of God: "Let it be to me according to your word" (Luke 1:38).

This union of divine and human freedom secures in the maiden of Nazareth a hope that will be fixed forever on God's words to her. From this moment on Mary's life will be completely sustained by the Incarnate Word, her child, who will come into the world as the tangible expression of God's love. Mary's child will embody the mutual freedom that has enabled her to become God's handmaid. Jesus is God the Father's commitment to Mary, and he will be forever the fruit of her hopefulness.

By her response to the archangel Mary is giving herself not only to the Father but also to the Son, the Word, who will determine in real, practical, substantial ways the unfolding of her life, even as he did at the moment of her conception. Mary is not merely submitting herself to a plan or an agenda; she is submitting herself to the Trinity. Her response, coming as it does after the unbelievable statement of the archangel, is Mary's "I do" to the Trinity.

This is the first great revelation of the Trinity in the New Testament, a moment from which we can understand rightly the whole of revelation. At this point Mary is no longer speaking just to the archangel; she is speaking to the divine Mystery, to the God who, through her and with her, will now be able to show himself as Father, Son and Holy Spirit.

This is the moment Lucifer feared, the moment against which he defined himself. This woman is his archenemy, the one of whom God said, "I will put enmity between you and the woman, / and between your seed and her seed" (Genesis 3:15). The simple, honest, heartfelt words of God's humble handmaid undo his grand rebellion.

Mary's life will never be the same. The Holy Spirit consummates God's love for her and her love for God, completing the work begun in her at the moment of her sinless conception.

Mary's gift of self confirms the fact that holiness is more than an absence of sin; it is the work of the Holy Spirit in those who willingly embrace their vocations. It is the experience of living one's humanity in all its fullness, living as God intended. Mary, immaculately conceived and therefore sinless, still longed to be completed in God. She lived utterly open to God's will, believing that her humanity would be fulfilled in him. Born in grace, Mary is at this moment forever wedded to grace, become one with grace.

The child conceived in her womb will be "the Son of the Most High" (Luke 1:32) and "the Son of God" (Luke 1:35). The prophetic words of Gabriel—"He will be great,...and the Lord God will give to him the throne of his father David, / and he will reign over the house of Jacob for ever; / and of his kingdom there will be no end" (Luke 1:32–33)—only begin to celebrate the child's destiny. The Source of holiness will be the fruit of holiness, the dynamic effect of the Holy Spirit on the humanity of Mary. He will be the Father's total openness to Mary and to us.

The flesh from which Jesus takes his human life is different from all other human flesh. Jesus is the perfect expression of humanity fully receptive to the divine. What will be done in Mary is what God the Father wants for the human family: to experience the personal expression of his unconditional love. This is only possible because Mary trusts the Father enough to say, "Let it be to me according to your word."

What will "be" is a relationship that is as marvelous as it is mysterious. The bond that exists between the handmaid of God and her child has not been formed according to the order of nature; rather, nature is the means by which mother and child are able to express the real spiritual bond that God has established. Nature serves the spiritual, exactly as it should.

The relationship between Mary and her child goes beyond other mother-child relationships. It is deeper than what nature alone is capable of expressing. And because nature serves their unique spiritual-physical bond, all the ways in which a mother cares, nourishes, protects, comforts and helps her child to grow become the means by which Mary caresses what she most treasures, nourishes her hopefulness and protects what she believes. Through the reality of her maternity Mary will be able to continue giving herself to God.

Mary's child is a perfect icon of God's vulnerability to human freedom and of the creative and sustaining power of the Holy Spirit. He is the perfect icon too of the Father's love for the human family. Mary's child challenges everything humanity thought it knew about itself, about God, about the meaning and purpose of human fertility. Her child challenges human hearts to be open to him, the one through whom we have access to the Father. Mary's child is the in-the-flesh expression of the love of God, the perfect means of revealing the fatherhood of God. "He who has seen me has seen the Father," he will tell the apostle Philip (John 14:9).

God's word wasn't addressed to Mary in a partial or limited way or for this moment alone. God's word comes to

Mary in all its richness at this precise moment and for *all* time. God communicates to humanity through the child Mary will bear. Her child will grow "in wisdom and in stature, and in favor with God and man" (Luke 2:52) because of the unique relationship he shares with his mother.

Jesus' words will resonate with the authority that governs, directs and animates the life of his mother. When he speaks for God, it will be from the depths of his heart, not simply the vastness of his mind. His words will be holy because they will issue from a humanity that is, like his mother's, totally and completely open to the will of the Father.

Mary's submission to the Father is a triumph of her freedom. By stepping into the rich, incomprehensible possibilities of God, Mary allows herself to become a celestial expression. Her humanity, her virginity, her maternity, will be forever part of the language of the divine in its self-communication.

Mary is not "lost" in the divine Word to which she submits her life, nor is her voice silenced by the action and communication of God. Through the exercise of her freedom, all that is uniquely and personally "Mary" is assumed into the eternal discourse of love that is Father, Son and Holy Spirit. Mary becomes not simply a mother but, on the order of grace, "the mother of all living" (Genesis 3:20).

THE DRAMATIC EXCHANGE BETWEEN MARY AND THE ARCH-
angel Gabriel has been summed up well in her title "Mother
of God." This ancient theological formula remains an invitation and a challenge to all believers. Mary's vocation as
Mother of God invites us to consider our own human fulfillment within the light of God's particular plan for our lives.
In the call issued to each person, God the Father continues
to remain vulnerable to human freedom. Just as Mary freely
chose to embrace the Father's vulnerability through his plan
for her life, we too are invited to embrace the Father's plan
for us and unite our freedom with God's own.

Mary's vocation is the expansion of her being, not its
limitation. Similarly, the vocation God calls each one of us
to accept will not confine our lives; it will enhance and
expand them.

The Mother of God invites us to live and experience holiness in the uniqueness of our personalities as we place them
at the service of God. Holiness of life is not only a genuine
expression of walking in God's ways; it is also the radically
personal overshadowing of the Holy Spirit, which enables us
to live according to God's plan. The Holy Spirit is the
Father's guarantee that we can "be" in the world according
to God's word. The Spirit enables us to serve the Lord's plan

by providing for our individual spiritual, intellectual and personal needs.

The Mother of God stands as the great sign that loving and serving the Lord through one's vocation is not contrary to human existence but fulfills it. Embracing God's call offers us the chance to "taste and see that the LORD is good" (Psalm 34:8) right here and right now. It offers us the chance to know ourselves as God knows us, and it challenges us to accept the way marked out for us as truly the way of our delight. The Mother of God invites us to abandon ourselves to the unimaginable possibilities of God.

Mary's life as Mother of God offers a challenge to all who would reduce Christianity to ethics or morality. Mary was not content to spend her life in the sinlessness of her unique conception. This gift, a direct action on the part of God, was not the fulfillment of her life but only its beginning. With no prior thought of being a mother, Mary placed her feminine humanity within the care of the Almighty and lived in its entirety the love of God and neighbor that her son would preach as the greatest of commandments (see Matthew 22:36–40).

Christianity is not simply living without sin; it is an active and engaged love of God that must express itself as an active, attentive and engaged love of others. The Mother of God confirms charity as the greatest theological virtue and the greatest human activity. She challenges all Christians to love sacrificially, confidently trusting God to rightly order their humanity for this singular purpose.

By embracing her vocation, the Mother of God knew her love for God not only within her heart but also within the dynamic context of being wife, mother, cousin, friend, disciple, neighbor and even a guest at a wedding. Mary challenges us to accept the truth that salvation, eternal life and heaven are not a private undertaking worked out between one's self and God. By placing herself totally and completely at the service of God, Mary places even the physically most intimate and personal parts of her being in the loving care of God as a gift for others. She challenges us to place ourselves physically and spiritually at the service of God and consequently at the service of our neighbor.

The Mother of God invites all believers to accept their own vocations in order to be open to reality in all its positive goodness. She invites us to add our voices to hers in giving expression to the longing in creation for its completeness in God (see Romans 8:22–23). She therefore challenges us to cooperate with reality as it journeys toward its perfection in God. The title "Mother of God" affirms God's original estimation of his creation: "God saw everything that he had made, and behold, it was very good" (Genesis 1:31).

Mary's vocation is like a sacrament in the sense that her virginal maternity is an outward sign, instituted by God to give grace. It demands that we let go of any preconceptions of God that would downplay what he has accomplished in her and limit what he is capable of accomplishing in us. It opens us to a new awareness of the relationship between body and spirit, the union of our very selves with the divine.

Mary's freedom, united with the Father, begs us to let go of personal fears and misconceptions about self and risk the wonder and the splendor of living openly and only for God. She urges us to unite our freedom with the freedom of God that comes to us in the flesh, in the person of the Son. She longs to have us willingly embrace the challenges of our personal vocations. Let us follow her example and allow the Holy Spirit to bring her son into the reality of the everyday circumstances of our lives. For she is an eternal sign that with God all things are possible.

PART TWO
Our Lady of Victories

Mary arose and went with haste into the hill country, to a city of Judah, and she entered the house of Zechariah and greeted Elizabeth. And when Elizabeth heard the greeting of Mary, the child leaped in her womb; and Elizabeth was filled with the Holy Spirit and she exclaimed with a loud cry, "Blessed are you among women, and blessed is the fruit of your womb! And why is this granted me, that the mother of my Lord should come to me? For behold, when the voice of your greeting came to my ears, the child in my womb leaped for joy. And blessed is she who believed that there would be a fulfilment of what was spoken to her from the Lord." And Mary said,

"My soul magnifies the Lord,
and my spirit rejoices in God my Savior,
for he has regarded the low estate of his handmaiden.
For behold, henceforth all generations will call me
blessed;
for he who is mighty has done great things for me,
and holy is his name.
And his mercy is on those who fear him
from generation to generation.
He has shown strength with his arm,
he has scattered the proud in the imagination of their
hearts,
he has put down the mighty from their thrones,
and exalted those of low degree;
he has filled the hungry with good things,

and the rich he has sent empty away.

He has helped his servant Israel,

in remembrance of his mercy,

as he spoke to our fathers,

to Abraham and to his posterity for ever."

And Mary remained with her about three months, and returned to her home. (Luke 1:39–56)

NEARLY ALL THE WAYS IN WHICH THE CHURCH AND HER members have come to refer to the Mother of God have been taken from the language of Scripture. The use of key terms as descriptive of Mary and her role in salvation history is meant to help the faithful understand this important woman of faith. The popular Litany of Our Lady offers us many such terms, such as "Mother of Good Counsel," "Mirror of Justice," "Seat of Wisdom," "Mystical Rose," "Tower of David," and "Help of Christians."[1] These terms draw attention to Mary and her life of virtue and indicate the place she occupies in the fulfillment of God's promises to his chosen people. The litany is a great tool for meditation. Mary certainly does not need us to sing her praises, but she allows her life to be a way into a greater appreciation of what God has accomplished for those who love him. Unfortunately, some titles of Mary can be unintentionally misleading. Some the church has rejected—such as the title "Virgin Priest"— because they are contrary to the faith. The church is careful that the words used to honor Mary do not overshadow the person and role of her son. The one who saves should never be confused with the woman who gave birth to him. Mary remains bound to the ministry of redemption, but she is not the redeemer.

The title Our Lady of Victories too would seem somewhat misleading. On the surface it appears as if Mary is being honored for some great accomplishment. One could perhaps surmise from this title an attitude toward the Mother of God that places her uncomfortably close to a position that only her son can occupy. Jesus alone is the victor over sin and death. No one but God can undo what was done by original sin.

Since the church allows the use of this honorific title of Mary, it is important that the nature of this victory be clarified and explained. The surest way to proceed toward such a goal is to begin by recalling that all titles of Mary are related to her vocation as the Mother of God. What she consented to do and to become for God the Father is the reference for all that the church teaches and claims about her.

Perhaps the greatest of Mary's words recorded in Scripture are those of the Magnificat, the prayer of praise she utters at her reception into the home of Elizabeth. The language of this heartfelt outburst reveals that the victory Mary understands her life to be is not a personal accomplishment but a triumph of God. Mary speaks these heartfelt words to her cousin Elizabeth, whom she "went with haste" to visit, moved by the charity that fills her life through the power of the Holy Spirit. The real drama in this loving encounter between Mary and Elizabeth is not simply what God has done for each woman but what each woman is able to see of themselves in one another.

Mary and Elizabeth are mirrors of each other's souls. The excitement of the encounter emerges from what they discover about themselves and the God who has favored them. It is from within this reflective experience that Mary gives voice to the victory that is the condition of her place in the world. The best way to understand why Mary is Our Lady of Victories is to listen to what she has to say.

ELIZABETH'S REPLY TO MARY'S GREETING MOST LIKELY catches Mary by surprise. Mary has not come just to share news of her astounding experience with the archangel Gabriel but to assist her cousin during her pregnancy and to celebrate this great gift and action of God. Mary's haste to see Elizabeth challenges the idea that God's privileges set people apart from others. What God has done for Mary is not for her alone. His actions have immense implications for all people.

Since Mary knows the exceptional circumstances of Elizabeth's pregnancy, it is easy to imagine that her greeting of Elizabeth might imitate the one Gabriel spoke to her in Nazareth, "Hail, full of grace, the Lord is with you!" (Luke 1:28). Elizabeth's question, "And why is this granted me, that the mother of my Lord should come to me?" (Luke 1:43), certainly mirrors Mary's initial feeling of "How can this be?" At the outset of this family reunion it is clear that these two women are united in faith just as they are through blood.

Two cousins, who surely have spent time together before, now face one another with wonder. I imagine their feelings to be not unlike those of the two disciples who will meet the resurrected Christ on the road to Emmaus (see Luke 24:13–35). Mary's heart and Elizabeth's heart "burn within" them. The Word of God has taken hold of their lives. By the power of the Holy Spirit they are no longer the persons they were before, not to themselves and not to each other.

The women stand transparent before one another, perfect mirrors for the divine action that now determines their places in the world. Elizabeth is not content simply to accept Mary's greeting but feels compelled to state plainly the mystery of divine favor that each of them has come to recognize: "Why is this granted me?" The joy they experience as a result of having opened their lives to the possibility of God extends to the child in Elizabeth's womb, who leaps at the sound of Mary's greeting (see Luke 1:44).

Elizabeth's words clarify the message of the archangel Gabriel and affirm what the Holy Spirit has accomplished both in her and in Mary. Her bold proclamation, inspired by the same Spirit who has overshadowed her cousin, pulls together the range of thoughts and emotions that were awakened in Mary at her encounter with the angel and encourage her to give full voice to all that she is holding inside.

Although Mary has come in order to help Elizabeth in her time of need, God provides in the person of Elizabeth someone in whom Mary can confide. Elizabeth's home is a secure and familiar environment in which a conversation between two women highly graced can take place. And Elizabeth's words are an open invitation for Mary to share what's burning inside her heart. It is as if Elizabeth is saying, "It's all right; I know."

Surely these words are comfort and encouragement for Mary. She finds herself able to share with another human being the victory of God that is the reality of her life. She can find the words to sing God's praises.

The first line of Mary's song leaves no room to doubt that God lies at the heart of her outburst. Her choice of words in no way implies that her life expands or enhances the divine being. Mary's song simply personalizes the words that begin Psalm 19, "The heavens are telling the glory of God; / and the firmament proclaims his handiwork." Mary recognizes that just as the heavens and the earth wordlessly proclaim the greatness of God, so also does her life. Her soul has become a lens through which others might better see God and his divine mystery. Mary's life is an instrument through which the world can see more clearly the Love that God is.

This first line of Mary's song describes God's vulnerability toward her in a profoundly personal way. God allows Mary to enable others to see and to consider him in a new light and from a new perspective. Her life hasn't added to, changed or perfected the life of God; she herself has done nothing and accomplished no victory. The free and total giving of herself to God has allowed God to radically affect her life and that of the world. Now her whole being is able to bring into better focus the dynamic loving that is the life of God. Mary's humanity is God's love-in-action enlarged for everyone to see.

Through the lens of Mary's sinless, feminine, virginal humanity, God has forever fixed himself before our eyes. Through the power of the Holy Spirit Mary has become an icon of divine love, a way for others to perceive the true nature of divinity her son reveals as a Trinitarian communion of love. Because Mary has already been assumed into this loving communion by freely consenting to God's plan, everything she is and all that she does become ways of perceiving the mystery as humanity never could have considered.

Although Mary is young and humble, her life now expresses the immensity and audacity of God's love for humanity. Standing before the mirror of her cousin's life, she is able to sum up what every person baptized into the life of her son is re-created to express: "My soul magnifies the Lord!" There are no more fitting words to express the truth of what her life has become by the power of his word at work in her through the action of the Holy Spirit.

The song Mary sings is called a victory song precisely because her life shows the personal and universal love of God on a grand scale. God achieves victory through Mary's submission to his freedom and by her willing embrace of his plan. Her openness to the divine initiative allows her distinctive human life to reveal new insights about the mystery of God. By accepting God's plan Mary becomes an expression of God's victory over human failing and the effects of original sin. Her submission to the Holy Spirit allows God to order the whole of her physiology, psychology and spirituality toward the divine plan of redemption.

God's victory will forever be manifested in the distinctive and particular details of Mary's life. Her history has become the history of God. God's victory is the union of humanity and divinity in a relationship of love that will never end. Mary can say with total and complete genuineness that her life magnifies the Lord. The song the Spirit has scored in her heart is the ultimate song of victory.

THE JOY THAT CAUSES ELIZABETH'S UNBORN CHILD TO LEAP IS the same as that which fills the soul of Mary. The intimate bond she shares with her cousin—and now with her cousin's child—is the work of the Spirit of God, who has overshadowed all three lives. "In the shelter of the Most High,...in the shadow of the Almighty" (Psalm 91:1), these people have been brought together. Their spiritual union gives rise to a joy that is more than simple contentment or emotional happiness; it is a joy that flows from the knowledge of God's saving action.

Mary's experience of the Holy Spirit is one of being totally free, for "where the Spirit of the Lord is, there is freedom" (2 Corinthians 3:17). Nothing can limit, constrict or hinder her, because she lives entirely for God. Her joy is the authentic expression of the full and abundant life that God wants for all human persons.

Mary has passed through the difference that has touched her life since the moment of her conception. All the ways in which God's creative initiative has marked her life as a woman and as a member of the chosen people have now fallen into place. Her sinless condition, far from being a burden, is revealed as the intricate care God has taken in order to free humanity from its slavery to sin and death.

Mary rejoices in the knowledge that God's ways are not the ways of men and women; he has been up to something in and for her. Her spirit is in such harmony with the Spirit of God that she is literally all joy.

Within the comfort of this intimately spiritual encounter with her cousin, we can sense that Mary feels completely at ease. The security of her bond with Elizabeth allows her to distill the experiences that have brought about her joy. This joy is not so much unbridled and exuberant as it is intensely refined, as her further words confirm. Mary must speak of the one who is responsible for her current state. The words of her song naturally "magnify" God.

Indeed, there is no real joy apart from God. The surest sign of knowing God and experiencing his love is the joy that infuses every facet of one's humanity. Because God is supremely personal, true knowledge of him and his love is never abstract or purely conceptual. Mary boldly proclaims that God's love is realized concretely in definitive moments and precise circumstances. Her song is a personal testimony that God's action is always directed at salvation.

Love, joy, God, salvation—all is intertwined for Mary, and so she speaks of God as Savior. She has personally experienced God's love and its effects. He indeed has saved her and not only from the stain of original sin. He has saved her from the desert wasteland that is human separation from Trinitarian communion. He has saved her from the waters unleashed by Satan in an attempt to sweep her from the face of the earth (see Revelation 12:13–16). God has saved her from a life of questioning whether or not her openness to him and her total gift of self have been found pleasing in his sight.

Mary's words do not merely borrow Scripture's words to form a theologically accurate picture of God's actions. Her personal experience of God is as substantial as the new human life growing within her womb. The Spirit has placed her within the courts of God, where "a day...is better than a thousand elsewhere" (Psalm 84:10). Mary serves there at the pleasure of the King, and her place with him is a sign of the victory he has achieved in her life.

This noble state doesn't isolate Mary from others but draws her ever more toward them in the hope that where she is they may be also. The court of God is not closed to those over whom he rules; it has been opened to them in a new way. The banquet God sets is ready, and the Lady of his courts throws open the doors of the banquet hall. God's Son will now go and bring in all who have been invited. He wants all his subjects to join the Queen Mother at court.

The salvation God has won for Mary will be physical as well as spiritual. Her body will bear the means of accomplishing God's victory. In her we see the expression of the mystery of God's love that only a woman can give: the physical nourishment and bringing forth of life—in her case, the Life of the world. Mary brings forth the very Word who orders and directs her life. Through the power of the Holy Spirit, salvation takes bodily form.

Mary sings of God's victory in a humanity being made whole. She sings from the depths of the royal communion into which her life has been assumed and of the unity of spirit she shares, even physically, with Elizabeth and her child. Her words form the first liturgical song of the new covenant, describing what lies at the heart of the Christian dispensation: God's victory over sin and death. In the grace of this encounter, joy is born into the world through the noble handmaid of Nazareth, "who believed that there would be a fulfilment of what was spoken to her from the Lord" (Luke 1:45).

CHAPTER TEN
"HE HAS REGARDED THE LOW ESTATE OF HIS HANDMAIDEN"

THE WORDS OF MARY'S SONG ARE MORE THAN A REFRAIN FOR greeting Elizabeth. Mary's words give form to what God has accomplished for her and shape the way we should understand the expression of God's love. The regard that Mary describes is not benign tolerance, condescending affection or feigned interest, nor is it self-absorbed benevolence seeking to reaffirm its generosity by seeing to the needs of others.

The favor to which Mary's life has been exposed is the active concern of the almighty and ever-living God. Mary triumphantly declares that God's favor does not tolerate distance and separation but seeks to eliminate them. God refuses to be silent before anything that would prohibit, limit, lessen or smother human life and human fulfillment. Mary knows divine favor as love in its greatest and most comprehensive expression; she knows that God has nothing to gain and everything to give. She knows that God's favor is the real experience of his love, which reaches toward us before we are formed in our mother's womb (see Jeremiah 1:5).

God looks toward us and favors us that we might know ourselves as he knows us. "Draw near to me, hear this," he says through the prophet Isaiah. "I have not spoken in secret" (Isaiah 48:16). From the beginning he openly communicates his divine countenance in numerous and varied ways. He desires that our "peace...[be] like a river, / and [our] righteousness like the waves of the sea" (Isaiah 48:18).

Mary grew up knowing that one could not look upon the face of God and live; the human heart cannot, of itself, bear the weight of such love. The fact that she can sing in the face of God's arresting gaze is a result of God's having acted upon her at the moment of her conception. Her sinlessness, the difference that set her apart from the rest of her race, was the divine love's preparation for her to one day bear the full weight of his favor. She now bears this weight in her womb. Mary has given herself to God's favor, and God has respected her self-giving and transformed it wonderfully.

The favor of God has borne fruit in the life of this trusting handmaiden. Mary's child, conceived entirely in grace, will become the living sign of the divine favor. God's own Son has been conceived in an active freedom, more dynamic than mere self-surrender. The child Mary bears takes human life through her embrace of God's favor and embodies God's victory.

Through the mutual subjugation of God and this woman, divine favor enters human history in a definitive and unrepeatable way. In order to appreciate fully God's love-in-the-flesh, in order to appreciate Jesus fully, one also must know this woman. God looks at her with a view to all human persons. Mary sees in the favor of God's glance an opportunity not simply to experience his love in the definitive way of giving birth but also to give her life as a gift on behalf of all men and women.

Mary's lowliness is the truth about her humanity before the awesome wonder and power of God. It is rooted in the nothingness out of which all things came to be. No one can stand on equal footing with the God of all creation. Mary knows herself to be radically other than God.

But Mary also knows that the divine favor, which has fixed its gaze upon her, can change the condition of her existence. Her lowliness becomes a statement of God's victory insofar as the divine favor holds her in its loving glance. God respects the initial gift of self her virginity signifies, and he unites her fertility with his own generative power, thereby transforming Mary's lowliness in a miraculous way. This is consistent with God's saving action throughout Israel's history: "Though the LORD is high, he regards the lowly" (Psalm 138:6).

Our Lady of Victories is the spokeswoman of humanity held captive by God's love, of humanity no longer separated from the God of creation. Humanity has been pulled from the nothingness into which it slid as a result of original sin, a lowliness Mary never knew personally but observed in the darkness of the world that surrounded her. Our Lady of Victories is a triumph of that love that has looked past human weakness and seen into the heart of the human family.

CHAPTER ELEVEN
"Henceforth All Generations Will Call Me Blessed"

The day of encounter between Mary and Elizabeth, related by blood and now intimately bound through faith, is a "day which the Lord has made" (Psalm 118:24). The creative activity of the Father has expressed itself in the generation of two new human lives. He has changed the way Mary and Elizabeth see themselves, one another and God. This new day, which the Lord has made through his sending of the Holy Spirit, will mark all of creation. It not only looks ahead to the end of the week, to the "new heaven and...new earth" of which Saint John will speak (Revelation 21:1); it also stretches back into the past, in particular into the history of Mary's people.

Israel's story is no longer one of a people's failure to live up to the unconditional fidelity of God. We can see its history now in light of God's desire to unite all people to him by providing them the means to share his very life. His actions in the past were not isolated victories over those who sought Israel's destruction; rather they were strategic movements ordered toward this new week of creation. Once more the Spirit will go forth, this time to "make all things new" (Revelation 21:5).

God has been preparing humanity to hear and to accept the great Word of his love, now come to live among us. This new day vindicates God's activity in the past even as it looks to God's activity in the future.

Mary recognizes that this new day—which she, Elizabeth and their children share—is a day of favor, a day of blessing. Their overwhelming experience of God causes Mary to sing prophetically of the countless lives that its light will change. These future generations will indeed call her blessed because of what God has accomplished in her and through her on behalf of humanity: the incarnation of his only begotten Son.

Mary is blessed because she "believed that there would be a fulfilment of what was spoken to her from the Lord" (Luke 1:45). This is not divine affirmation for completing a task or fulfilling a duty. The blessing of God is the intimate experience of the life of his Son, an experience available to all those who likewise will place themselves confidently within the Word of God's love and follow it. God's favor, God's blessing, has flesh and blood. All generations will call Mary blessed because she bears God's blessing and literally gives it life.

These generations will affirm not only God's love for the world but also the power of human freedom when it unites itself with the freedom and the possibilities of God. Calling Mary blessed is cheerful recognition that she is the Lady of Victories, the humble handmaiden whose free and total submission to the Word of God enables God to set his people free.

On this new day of creation God's love is expressed in the world in a way that no one in the past could have foreseen—and that many in the future will not accept. Mary's life will reflect the light of victory that now has dawned upon the human family. "Our Lady of Victories" is the appropriate recognition of the blessing she has received within her womb. It is the appropriate appellation for the favor she has accepted on behalf of all men and women. It is a statement of confidence and hope for all those who will receive the Word of God and follow him.

The dramatic events that unite Mary with her cousin give voice to God's saving love and invite all people to share the blessing and live within the light of this new day. Our Lady of Victories invites us to sing with her, "This is the day which the Lord has made; / let us rejoice and be glad in it" (Psalm 118:24).

CHAPTER TWELVE
"He Who Is Mighty Has Done Great Things for Me, and Holy Is His Name"

In the light of all that has taken place recently in her life and the life of her cousin, Mary's insight penetrates to the heart of God's plan. Her words speak of God's love in a highly personal way. God's saving activity is addressed to humanity. This salvation comes "in the likeness of man" and by way of a man, and therefore it directly touches our humanity.

Mary sings of the highly personal character of God's saving love, because this love has completely reordered her life. God desires salvation for all men and women, and he will touch intimately each life that accepts this gift.

Mary's song is filled with joy because God has won salvation *for* her. She can only describe God's saving love in terms of the way in which that love has acted in and upon her life. Mary declares with utter sincerity and unabashed clarity that God is her personal Lord and Savior. Salvation is as real as the child growing in her womb.

In lauding the "great things" God has done, Mary is thinking of the whole of her life. Salvation describes the way she was conceived, it explains the way she has lived her life for God, and it fuels the desires of her heart. Salvation is hers as a member of God's chosen people. And now she is pregnant with the source of salvation, the Son of the Most High. What great things the Most High has done.

Perhaps Mary does not list all the "great things" because every part of her life is an expression of God's greatness; everything in her life has been charged with his grandeur. Mary's selfless response to the gift of God's love has filled her life in ways she never before imagined. Her eyes are open to behold the wonders of God's love working so decisively yet so sensitively within the fabric of her existence. Mary is living proof of the power of God's generosity.

The great things that God has done specifically for Mary verify the "holiness" of his name and draw Mary closer to him. His work is attuned to the uniqueness of her situation. "How majestic is your name in all the earth!" Mary has prayed (Psalm 8:1, 9)—not because God is aloof or distant, and not even because he is so much greater than that which his hands have made. She knows that God's name is holy because he is "omnipersonal," closer to us than we are to ourselves.

Mary isn't afraid to speak the name of God, for she is proclaiming the splendor, the glory, the wonder of Love himself. Mary has physically experienced love not as an attribute or an activity of God but as his very nature. The name *God* is not simply a way of conceptualizing that which is the origin of all that exists; rather it is the name of the ultimate personal reality. He reveals himself in the great things he does for those who open themselves to him. Mary's song links holiness with the divine name in a new way. The Israelites were so aware of the holiness of God's name as revealed to Moses (see Exodus 3:14) that they would not speak it.

Holiness became associated with God in a way that put it beyond what humanity could hope to experience. Through the great things God has done, Mary understands holiness as the action of God at work through, with and in her humanity. Holiness is the effect of God's fulfilling the humanity of the one who has opened his or her life to his love.

Through the great things God has done, Mary knows that her life too is holy. She is who God created her to be; God has fulfilled her humanity. God has not withdrawn from her, nor does he wish to withdraw from us. He wants all men and women to live within and to be fulfilled by his own life.

The holiness of God's name is not meant to frighten us and make us cower in our fragility, vulnerability and sin. The holiness of God's name is an invitation to draw closer to him and to open our lives to the Love who can do great things for us.

The Almighty is the guarantor of the title "Our Lady of Victories." The nuances of divine love working on the singular details of Mary's life form the collective victory of God's love in action. Mary has been set up "with the princes of his people" (Psalm 113:8) through the intricate work of divine love.

This is the love Mary freely embraces, the Love that now has a name and literally grows inside her. The great things of God are Love's triumph and living signs of Love's victory. Mary is forever Our Lady of Victories, a living testament to the highly personal attentiveness of God's love, which accomplishes great things for those who believe.

CHAPTER THIRTEEN
"His Mercy Is on Those Who Fear Him From Generation to Generation"

Through the overshadowing of the Holy Spirit Mary has come to understand that God has been acting not only in her life but in the lives of all people, even from the moment of the original sin of the first human couple. Satan did not overcome God's desire that humanity share his life. God has been working within the history of fallen humanity with a view toward restoring what was lost on that fateful day in the Garden of Eden.

God, of course, is not fooled by mankind's will to power. He has been working despite the world's limitations, "the lust of the flesh and the lust of the eyes and the pride of life" (1 John 2:16). Adam and Eve may have felt that they knew what was best for them, but the love of God was not silenced by their elevation of self and their act of disobedience. Mary seems to look backward in the light of her own moment of grace and see how God has been working "from generation to generation" (Luke 1:50).

God has not sentenced humanity to a destiny without hope and purpose, without eternal significance. God's love, rather than being diminished by the actions of the first human couple, came to be spoken in a language that only the ailing can understand: the language of mercy. As Mary's son will remind us, "those who are well have no need of a physician, but those who are sick" (Luke 5:31).

In a world disordered by sin, a world in which nature continues to long for its completion because man's selfishness has impeded nature's journey toward perfection, the language of God is mercy. The gift of love is a gift of mercy. To fallen humanity love and mercy are one and the same. God's love is merciful, and God is merciful because God is love.

In the light of her graced encounter with Elizabeth, Mary can see that God's love has been reaching toward and acting on behalf of humanity in spite of sin. God has been merciful in every generation because God is always fully God. Love may have been rejected in the Garden of Eden, but it wasn't put to death. From that moment on God has been working to show definitively that "his mercy endures for ever" (Psalm 118:1). Mary now bears within her body the definitive expression of God's love as mercy toward a fallen world. Her child is Love in the flesh; her child is divine mercy incarnate.

From generation to generation God has been preparing the human family for a reconciliation that will last through all ages. The covenant with Noah, the call of Abraham, the covenant at Sinai, the throne of David, the sending of the prophets—these were all ways in which God was working within human history to express the depth of his love in the context of a redemptive relationship. Mercy has touched every age and all peoples, particularly the chosen people. God established his covenant with them so that all nations could come to know him. He longs for all people to share in a personal relationship with him, a relationship that he gives freely to those who will give themselves freely to him in return.

The way to experience this mercy is the same pathway that leads to wisdom: "The fear of the LORD is the beginning of wisdom, / and the knowledge of the Holy One is insight" (Proverbs 9:10). Mary knows this "fear of the Lord" not as something that cripples the human spirit before the power of the Almighty but as the wonder and awe that come from recognizing God's incomprehensible love for us. Those who realize that life is only possible because God has called us into being stand in fear before this astounding truth. The fear of the Lord is the acceptance of human finitude, human limits and human failure before the One who alone can offer total human fulfillment.

Those who fear the Lord know that life is his gift, as is the world in which we live. They recognize that "the heavens are telling the glory of God; and the firmament proclaims his handiwork" (Psalm 19:1). All things praise the Lord of the universe. Those who fear the Lord are humbled by the goodness and beauty of reality. This sense of wonder and awe, this honest disposition before such grandeur, opens us to the experience of God's mercy, to the tangible sense of being loved and cared for by the Author of all that is.

Our Lady of Victories is the champion of God's love as mercy. She is the sentinel of God's activity within history to reunite humanity with himself. Our Lady of Victories is a sign of contradiction to those who live as if all was lost on the day that Adam and Eve traded friendship with God for individual autonomy. Our Lady of Victories is a noble expression of God's unrelenting presence within a history marred by sin and lives fallen from grace.

Our Lady of Victories confirms the fact that the fear of the Lord is the first stage of wisdom. Those who walk in the ways of the Lord, she says, are happy (see Psalm 1:1–2). God can exalt the fallen, wounded human spirit. Truly "his mercy endures for ever" (Psalm 136).

FOR GENERATIONS THE PEOPLE OF ISRAEL HAD LOOKED TO THE Lord to be their strength. Often God had extended his arm toward them, especially to help them overcome their enemies. "Because of the greatness of your arm, they are as still as stone," the Israelites sang after Pharaoh's army drowned in the Red Sea (Exodus 15:16). The "Lord's right arm" was synonymous with God's power to protect and to safeguard his people. "His right hand and his holy arm have gotten him victory," Psalm 98 tells us.

Mary knows well that God's arm has been stretched out toward his people from generation to generation. She now immerses herself within the litany of God's saving love and lauds the "strength of God's arm" with vibrant urgency. Now is a new time of God's action, and he is out to conquer the enemy once and for all. This is a woman who knows that "the kingdom of God is at hand" (Mark 1:15).

God reached out his saving arm toward the young handmaiden of Nazareth, and she took hold of it. She incorporates the image here at the dawn of Christianity with a significance that transcends the historical. The strength of God's arm has raised her to the heights that God longs to share with all his people. The strength of God's arm is Mary's humanity wholly ordered to the divine plan of redemption. The strength of God's arm is Mary's virginal fertility, her confident femininity, her virtuous maternity and her chaste matrimony. The strength of God's arm is no anachronism from the past but the destiny of all of humanity.

The strength of God's arm scatters the proud, those who claim that they alone determine what is good and true and beautiful for their lives. The strength of God's arm pushes aside the deceptions of the serpent deemed "more subtle than any other wild creature" (Genesis 3:1). God's victorious love challenges all that was learned in eating from the Tree of Knowledge of Good and Evil, when the serpent told Adam and Eve that they would "be like God" (Genesis 3:5).

Through the power of God's arm, Mary has become an icon, a living flesh-and-blood picture of what God has not only imagined but also accomplished for Mary and for our salvation. Her portrayal in the Scriptures, as well as her pictures and statues today, continue to scatter those whose imaginations cannot conceive of the depths of God's creative initiative as it has been written into the story of this woman's life. Mary is the strength of God's arm for all generations, a perfect expression of victorious love.

God exercises his strength with respect to the woman whose *fiat* makes possible the human conception of his eternal Son. God did not send his Son into the world as a terrifying spirit or some monstrous figure. Rather, "the Word became flesh and dwelt among us, full of grace and truth" (John 1:14). God undertakes the victory of his love in a way that all men and women can understand and touch and love.

"We cannot but speak of what we have seen and heard," Jesus' disciples will say (Acts 4:20). What humanity could not imagine, God has conceived in the womb of this woman.

God scatters the proud to clear the way for the victorious entrance of his Son. Mary becomes the gateway by which the King of Glory decisively enters into the history of the human family (see Psalm 24). Her genealogy secures her child to the strength of God's arm as it was revealed in the past. Now her child secures her to the strength of God's arm as it will be revealed in the future.

The human heart could never have conceived that "God so loved the world that he gave his only-begotten Son, that whoever believes in him should not perish but have eternal life" (John 3:16). This is the extent of God's love that Jesus will manifest in his walk on the earth. God has shown Mary the true strength of his arm in making a way for the Son of the Most High to come into the world. Everything God has done has been oriented toward the moment of this woman and her child.

Mary's graced encounter with Elizabeth enables her to see what God is doing for those who love him. She can see with clarity in the light of this privileged moment with her cousin precisely because her heart is pure and her imagination unsullied by the poison from the fruit of the Tree of Knowledge of Good and Evil. For it takes a humble, contrite heart to recognize that fruit as poison.

Our Lady of Victories champions humility and honesty because she knows that "the pure in heart...shall see God" (Matthew 5:8). Our Lady of Victories is the noble escort of those who walk on the pathway cleared by the strength of

God's arm. She terrifies those who wish to control and dominate others, even as she is mocked by those who continue to gorge themselves on the poisonous fruit of the "Tree".

Our Lady of Victories is the sentinel of God's love, the untiring witness to the triumph of divine love over human arrogance and sin. Our Lady of Victories is God's pledge that the strength of his arm will never depart from the history of man, specifically from the history of those who accept her son and seek to follow in his ways. "Our Lady of Victories" is a fitting tribute to the truth of Mary's song: God "has shown strength with his arm, / he has scattered the proud in the imagination of their hearts" (Luke 1:51).

CHAPTER FIFTEEN
"He Has Put Down the Mighty From Their Thrones, and Exalted Those of Low Degree"

These words of Mary's song strike at the heart of the disorder caused by original sin. In the elevation of self over and against God and neighbor, human relations became charged with destructive tension. The relationships between men and women, individuals and communities, no longer expressed the communion that even nature was ordered to express. Individual autonomy became the driving force of human endeavors. God's desire that "they may be one" (see John 17:11) was thwarted, resulting in a fragmentation that human ingenuity and political creativity could not overcome.

The throne to self put up on that fateful day in the Garden of Eden has proved to be as unsteady and untenable as the Israelites' golden calf. Atop this throne men and women have tremulously perched, all the while looking for a way down, though too afraid to jump. The throne of the mighty is this self-exaltation that has disordered the world and separated the human family from God.

Mary, who feels within her body the saving love of God, sees clearly that no one but God can turn such a throne into a footstool. All the men and women around her are the mighty who have been cast down, for all are infected with the sin of Adam. Yet just as surely they are "those of low degree" whom God longs to lift up.

The low degree of humanity is the direct result of the choice Adam and Eve made to govern themselves rather than adhere to God's word. Under the burden of the feckless mighty, people have suffered, have been enslaved and have died. The elevation of self bankrupted the richness of the life that God created to be "very good." Those who recognize the truth and reality of the human condition long for a better life, for happiness without end.

Mary understands the longing of all human hearts, even when hidden beneath the veneer of power. "My God, I seek you, / my soul thirsts for you; / my flesh faints for you, / as in a dry and weary land where no water is" (Psalm 63:1). Mary has experienced what it means to be lifted up by God, and she understands this favor as something God longs to do for all men and women.

Mary sings the truth of the human condition even as she sings prophetically of her son. As Simeon will tell Mary and Joseph, the child she bears is "set for the fall and rising of many in Israel" (Luke 2:34). Her child is the one who will cast down and the one who will raise up. He will bear in his flesh the desire of the Father to undo the low degree of fallen humanity—indeed, to exalt humanity. He will put to rest the suffering inflicted by the mighty and raise the human family to union with God.

Mary's words are born of her desire that all men and women be saved. She wants the Lord to cast down the mighty not out of spite but out of genuine love, for she knows that "the Lord reproves him whom he loves" (Proverbs 3:12). Mary wants anyone who is burdened by the weight of self-exaltation to fall in order that God might raise them up. She cries out for the saving power of God to shatter the illusions of sin and heal the disintegration of the human family. She clamors for the freedom and salvation that can come only in accepting God's love, which will be expressed ultimately in the casting down and the raising up of her son.

In the grace of this encounter with Elizabeth, Mary intuitively expounds the mission of her child. She wants everyone to rejoice with her because what was lost—personal and intimate communion with God—has been found (see Luke 15:8–10) through the tremendous saving action of the Most High.

Our Lady of Victories stands at the center of what God accomplished in our past and what he will accomplish in our future. She stands outside of time, looking upon the human family from beneath the shelter of the Spirit's wing. Our Lady of Victories is the Spirit's promise of a heaven and earth no longer disordered by sin. She is humanity exalted according to the plan of God. She is the living symbol of the union of man and woman, of the individual and the community, of the human person with God.

Our Lady of Victories sees the thrones of the mighty destroyed, their royal chambers ruined, their fragile egos shattered. She knows that all who are trampled and manipulated will be raised up to take their place in the palace of the King. She offers tribute to God for the lengths to which he will go to raise up all who are fallen.

CHAPTER SIXTEEN
"He Has Filled the Hungry With Good Things, and the Rich He Has Sent Empty Away"

When Mary's people wandered in the desert toward the Promised Land, God rained from heaven manna, "a fine, flake-like thing, fine as hoarfrost on the ground," which Moses informed them was "the bread which the LORD has given you to eat" (Exodus 16:14, 15). He also sent quails to them in the evening for meat (see verse 13). During their forty-year pilgrimage God provided this food for the Israelites every day, and he also responded to their needs for water (see Exodus 17:1–7; Numbers 20:2–13; Deuteronomy 8:15).

God had freed the Israelites from their slavery in Egypt and protected them from Pharaoh's chariots and charioteers. Now he provided them with food and water as they worked their way toward "a good and broad land, a land flowing with milk and honey" (Exodus 3:8). When the people sought the Lord, "the LORD [delivered] them out of all their troubles" (Psalm 34:17).

Even when Israel's patience wore out because of the journey, God continued to satisfy their longings. The people would at times complain about the provisions they received from the hand of God, yet he never abandoned them. Many times their disobedience caused them distress. "Then they cried to the LORD in their trouble, / and he delivered them from their distress" (Psalm 107: 6, 13, 19, 28). Time and time again God proved himself to be a good Father to his daughter Israel.

Mary's words echo the past, but the Holy Spirit gives new life to those words. She is not singing of days long ago, of memories made sacred by God's loving care. The inspired words of Scripture—ever ancient, ever new—are flush with the blood of the child growing in her womb. Paternal love remains the abiding hallmark of God's relationship with the chosen people.

God satisfies our hunger with a new manna. He delivers us from the hardship and distress of sin and the anguish of death. Mary is proclaiming something remarkable about her child: he is God "[filling] the hungry with good things" (Luke 1:53). As "the true bread from heaven" (John 6:32), Jesus fleshes out the actions of God in the past.

Mary understands the history of God's people in the light of the grace that fills her life and the life of her cousin. She knows that the fruit of God's plan—her child—is the reason behind everything God has done to satisfy the longings of his people. In the beauty of this moment, Mary sees the goodness of the Lord as the child in her womb. Her song celebrates the fact that God satisfies the longing of the human heart for righteousness, justice and peace in a way that no religious system, no ruling power and no amount of money ever could.

Mary's thanksgiving to God makes her song fully "eucharistic." She is giving thanks to God even as she looks forward to the day when the poor will have their fill of the

Bread of Life. This is the Bread that fully satisfies, that truly gives life. Jesus will state clearly, "Your fathers ate the manna in the wilderness, and they died. This is the bread which comes down from heaven, that a man may eat of it and not die" (John 6:49–50).

"O taste and see that the LORD is good!" (Psalm 34:8). Mary truly has tasted the goodness of the Lord by receiving within her body the Father's only begotten Son. Jesus is Mary's communion with the Father, and she senses that Jesus will be communion with the Father for the entire human family. Having received the real presence of God, her life overflows with the good things God longs to give to all those who seek him (see Psalm 34:10).

At the same time Mary knows that many will loathe the food that God sets before them. Many will fly from this meal because they have gorged themselves on food that will never last. They have satiated anxious needs, fulfilled selfish desires and renounced the goodness of creation in favor of its utility. These rich will be sent away because they've left no room for the choice food and rich wine that God wants to set before his people. Sickened by sin and guilt, the rich are left hollow and malnourished.

In their places will be sitting those who take pure and honest delight in the goodness of everything God has made. They are those who know that the ordinances of the Lord are sweeter than honey. They appreciate the heavenly food that the Lamb graciously offers.

Our Lady of Victories is hostess at the banquet of the Lamb. She is the first to have eaten with delight from this heavenly feast. She is the noble matron of the Eucharist because she shares life with the Lamb of Sacrifice. She feeds on the Bread that she likewise offers.

Our Lady of Victories is a pledge of the good things that God longs to give those who hunger and thirst for righteousness. She is the assurance that the lowly and downhearted will have their fill and be glad. She stands waiting to welcome us into the New Jerusalem, the eternal city that is the fitting dwelling place for all men and women.

Our Lady of Victories affirms the Eucharist's power to give eternal life to all who believe, to wipe away the guilt of the human family. She is the custodian of the real presence, the constant reminder that truly God is with us. She is the wisest of virgins, for she kept her lamp burning even when it seemed as if the Groom was delayed in coming (see Matthew 25:1–13). Now she moves within a banquet hall well-lit, not by the light of the sun or oil lamps but by the light of the Bridegroom. And the Father of the Groom has provided the good things necessary for all invited guests—young and old—to make merry and to dance, to eat and to have their fill.

THE FINAL PHRASE OF MARY'S INSPIRED SONG COMES FROM within the bosom of time impregnated with the eternal. She is able to look from the vantage point of the God who remains outside of time. What has been remains fixed in the reality of the present moment. "With the Lord one day is as a thousand years, and a thousand years as one day" (2 Peter 3:8).

Mary has come to know that "I Am" is a name that encompasses the totality of the Trinity's eternal loving communion, even as the expressions of that communion punctuate space and time. The child Jesus, in the historical "now," is the Father's fulfillment of her people's hope for redemption. Her child is the real living presence of the Father's love, the real living presence that is the answer to Israel's prayers for mercy.

Standing outside of time insofar as she has been assumed into the loving communion of the Trinity, Mary can see that the help God has been giving to his people goes beyond the covenant with Noah, the call of Abraham, the Sinai covenant and the sending of the prophets. These are all different vantage points from which we can see the reality of divine love, though we never can perceive its totality. The help that God has extended to Israel is his revelation of the mystery of divine love from a multitude of profiles, in order that the mystery might be better known and understood. The past of her people is an expression of God's condescension to love the human family.

Mary sees these historical moments of God's care as the eternal communion that is each person's destiny. The deliverance is for each of us; the covenant is our covenant with God; the manna is our own. God loves his people all the time and in all places. Now God has found the perfect way to show what everything has been about. Mary's child is the physical expression of God's loving mercy.

The human memory is short. Jesus is a real Person, concrete, touchable. He will provide an unforgettable awareness of God's love and care.

The union of time and eternity expressed within this last line of Mary's song forms an outrageous claim: The Master comes to the aid of his servant. No other religion has ever been so bold. The various gods and goddesses of other peoples were not in the habit of aiding humanity unless it served their own purposes. The God of whom Mary sings is not a manipulative, angry or controlling deity who has his own purposes in mind. This is a God who helps his servants, who feeds and gives water, who fills up what is lacking and who does "great things." Mary's God acts only and always from love for his servant. "The remembrance of his mercy" is the eternal truth of his love temporally expressed.

From this inspired and eternal perspective Mary can see that God aids his servants in love, for love is the willingness to give oneself entirely to another. Not only does Mary know the depths of God's love, but she realizes that she is God's friend. Her Son, on the night before he dies, will tell his disciples, "You are my friends if you do what I command you" (John 15:14), confirming the truth of what his mother learned through grace.

God reached out to Abraham not simply in response to his prayer for children but in order that all nations might one day be gathered into friendship with God. Through the overshadowing of the Holy Spirit, Mary now knows what God has been about, and she attempts to unite all God's activity with the singular expression of her child. This activity must include Abraham, not only for religious and historical reasons but also because of the unique way in which Mary came to be with child.

Just as God's promise of offspring to Abraham transcended the biological, Mary knows that her maternity exists on the order of grace. She is a child of Abraham according to genealogy but more importantly according to the order of faith. In this communion of grace she can see the power of Abraham's yes to God and the implications of her own yes to him.

The *forever* that describes God's remembrance of love and redemption calls attention to both the ways in which God has acted and why God has acted at all. Mary can see her vocation as what God has determined to do not just at this particular moment in time but for all who will love him, in all times and all places.

Mary's vocation is the means by which God most suitably expresses his saving love. Just as the vocation of

Abraham opened the way for God to form Israel into a people, so Mary's vocation will bring these people and the people of all nations to God. The "forever" of God's mercy gives a decisive influence to each person's vocation. Those who embrace their call live within and give expression to the memorial of redemption.

Our Lady of Victories is the ultimate icon of Israel, for she is the ultimate model of what it means to be God's servant. Her noble character issues from the friendship she enjoys with the Master, who has shared with her everything he is about.

Our Lady of Victories brings forth the fulfillment of God's promises, the living memory of his eternal love. Living within the "eternal now" of God, she is a fixed point of reference for understanding just what it means to say that "God so loved the world" (John 3:16). She inspires vocations, bestowing from the noble treasury of her generous love the vitality that comes with saying yes to God.

THE GRACED MEETING WITH HER COUSIN ELIZABETH FIXES Mary's experience of God's plan for her life within the larger public arena of God's plan for her people and the whole of humanity. The meeting, precipitated by the work of the Holy Spirit, is a touching prelude to the dramatic historical events that will secure authentic human freedom as the antidote for the disorders caused by original sin.

In her victory song Mary gives praise to God for her experience of recent events within the community to which she and Elizabeth belong. She includes the context of the whole human family in her praise of God's love. Both she and Elizabeth know that what they have experienced at the hand of God is for more than themselves. Elizabeth's child will bring her and Zechariah "joy and gladness," but the angel also told Zechariah that "many will rejoice at his birth," and "he will turn many of the sons of Israel to the Lord their God" (Luke 1:14, 16). Gabriel has told Mary that her child will sit on "the throne of his father David, / and he will reign over the house of Jacob for ever" (Luke 1:32–33).

Mary and Elizabeth sense God's embrace of their femininity and his creative initiative within a global context. Each woman knows, in the communion of spirit that now binds them together, that to live for God one must live for those he loves. Mary and Elizabeth share within the unique conditions of their existence the revelation that a personal relationship with God means placing one's life at the service of the human family.

The Magnificat sings of God's triumph over the rupture in the harmony of the human family. The salvation growing within Mary's body will extend beyond juridical concepts like receiving a commuted sentence or even being pardoned. God's victory is not a matter of his looking the other way when confronted with human transgressions, simply ignoring human sinfulness because of his supreme benevolence. The salvation Mary has received bodily will extend to the depths of the human heart, enabling it to give real expression to the love out of which it was created and for which it is destined.

God's victory is conceived "in the flesh," in the lives of those baptized into Christ who have embraced God's love by accepting his plan for them. God's victory is the vocation to which he calls each person. God's victory is the wedding of the private with the public, the individual with the community and the sacred with the secular.

The noble character of Mary's victory hymn is born from God's conquest over the tragic consequences of the choice made in the Garden of Eden by the original human couple. The dignity that ennobles human life is our sharing with and participating in God's own life.

We can assume that Mary feels herself to be an entirely new person as a result of the angel's announcement. Her unique vocation comprises more than being with child; she is adorned with the graciousness that is the divine nature.

She looks at all of reality from a new view, from the kingdom heights to which God has lifted her. Mary expresses the victory that is God's raising of fallen humanity and bestowing upon it a dignity surpassing that which was lost through disobedience.

Mary's nobility is more than the restoration of the divine image in which all human beings have been created. Our Lady of Victories is the celebration of a full and vibrant humanity so in union with God that the soul can cry out, "It is no longer I who live, but Christ who lives in me; and the life I now live in the flesh I live by faith in the Son of God, who loved me and gave himself for me" (Galatians 2:20).

Our Lady of Victories underscores the distinctiveness of femininity in the revelation of God's love for humanity. God works within a human life without annihilating nature or that which is unique to the individual. Mary lives within the mystery of redemptive love, reminding us that victory is for every age and every time. By accepting the victory Christ has won for us, we move into intimate communion with all who love God, including Our Lady of Victories. We celebrate her life as an everlasting sign of the communion of life and love that is God's victory for us over sin and death.

PART THREE
MOTHER OF THE CHURCH

Now his parents went to Jerusalem every year at the feast of the Passover. And when he was twelve years old, they went up according to custom; and when the feast was ended, as they were returning, the boy Jesus stayed behind in Jerusalem. His parents did not know it, but supposing him to be in the company they went a day's journey, and they sought him among their kinsfolk and acquaintances; and when they did not find him, they returned to Jerusalem, seeking him. After three days they found him in the temple, sitting among the teachers, listening to them and asking them questions; and all who heard him were amazed at his understanding and his answers. And when they saw him they were astonished; and his mother said to him, "Son, why have you treated us so? Behold, your father and I have been looking for you anxiously." And he said to them, "How is it that you sought me? Did you not know that I must be in my Father's house?" And they did not understand the saying which he spoke to them. And he went down with them and came to Nazareth, and was obedient to them; and his mother kept all these things in her heart. (Luke 2:41–51)

S AINT PAUL REMINDS US THAT WE MUST SET OUR MINDS "ON things that are above" (Colossians 3:2), using the fixed terminology of our faith as a way of moving closer to the God who has shared himself with us. Throughout her life Saint Thérèse of Lisieux tried to do exactly this in her poetry, paintings and plays, in her personal letters to family and friends and in her autobiography. Saint Thérèse wanted to give herself fully to the church, not simply living the rigors of Carmel but also living in a real sense of fraternity with the entire body of Christ. The words of Saint Paul eventually led Saint Thérèse to define her life as love "in the heart of the Church."[1]

This should be the natural movement for every believer. Christ established the church to be the effective means by which people of all nations and all ages might experience his abiding presence and have real access to the Father. Mary embodies this truth of the church as does no other human being.

The Visitation already demonstrates that the work of the Holy Spirit is to gather people around the person of Christ. Mary's yes to the Father's plan has opened the door to the Spirit's work. In her meeting with Elizabeth and the unborn John the Baptist, the church is already being formed, for wherever the Spirit gathers people around the person of Christ, there is the church.

In what she teaches and how she makes Christ truly present in the world, the church is inextricably bound to the same Spirit by which Christ was able to be "born of woman" (Galatians 4:4) and enter into the history of the human family. The teachings of the church, as an integrated whole, convey the depths of God's love even as they serve as a treasury for personal and communal meditation. Although the truths of the faith can never be altered, eliminated or exhausted, over the centuries men and women like Saint Thérèse have added to this great treasury the fruits of their own reflections on the mystery of God's saving love. Through the inspiration of the Holy Spirit and the authority of the church, that which was initially entrusted to the apostles has been greatly enriched through personal devotion and ongoing contemplation.

By the middle of the third century the church, especially in the East, expressed through prayer and popular devotion a love for the mother of Jesus. Already her life was recognized as having significance for understanding just what it means to be the assembly of men and women gathered around Christ. The command to John at the foot of the cross, "Behold, your mother!" (John 19:27), was embraced by increasing numbers of the community of believers. By the fifth century it would be clear that Mary was not only the mother of Jesus but also the mother of all those who had been incorporated into his body, the church.

In recognizing Mary as Mother of the Church, the church has embraced Mary's role in salvation history as something more than an incidental historical moment or an interesting and inspiring theme. Her response to the Father's plan and her eternal loving communion with Jesus have naturally and supernaturally drawn her into the lives of those who "hear the word of God and do it" (Luke 8:21).

Mary knows well what it means to open the whole of oneself to the Father's will. Her openness unites her to the life of her son in a way that allows all members of the body of Christ to embrace her as their mother. For nearly sixteen hundred years the church has encouraged us to do just that.

CHAPTER TWENTY
"SON..."

S AINT LUKE COMPOSED HIS GOSPEL AS "AN ORDERLY ACCOUNT" that would provide Theophilus with certainty regarding the teachings that had been handed down by eyewitnesses and other ministers (see Luke 1:1–4). The first word that he records Mary speaking to Jesus resonates with the stated aim of the Gospel's author. Jesus is in fact Mary's son; she cannot be extricated from the certainty of the events of Christianity.

Mary's maternity binds her to the church. The communion she shares with us transcends the biological relationship between her and her son, which many Christians acknowledge, though some do not honor or celebrate it.

The fact that Luke has recorded this word *son* is significant, for thus he defines the movement from the narrative of the infancy of Jesus to that of his public ministry. While it is true that Jesus must be about the Father's work, this is not at the expense of the humanity he assumed from the woman of Nazareth and the authentic relationships that are part of his being human. Jesus will return and be obedient to his parents in all things precisely because the Father's plan incorporates the need for the boy to continue growing in "wisdom and in stature, and in favor with God and man" (Luke 2:52). Mary's word is a trumpet sound of the coming of the Son of Man.

Mary's statement of her personal relationship with Jesus is an integral part of the scene at the temple in Jerusalem. The church should treasure this word, for it reaches beyond the historical moment to anticipate the Father's bold proclamation that will signify the beginning of Jesus' public ministry, "This is my beloved Son" (Matthew 3:17; see Mark 1:11; Luke 3:22). Mary can say this too about the central figure of Saint Luke's Gospel.

Mary's word to Jesus in the presence of the learned teachers of the temple has its source in the same genuine astonishment she felt at her encounter with the archangel Gabriel and at the time of Jesus' circumcision. Mary's yes did not secure such a fixed place in God's plan that all sense of wonder was lost as that plan began to unfold. In freely subjecting herself to the Father's initiative, Mary did not become a passive spectator with full knowledge of the details concerning the life of her child. Rather, her life was one of continual surrender. Throughout her life God will call her to express ever more deeply her trust and confidence in him, the hope and joy of his providential care and the genuine peace of heart that flows from his paternal love.

So as Mother of the Church, Mary remains forever touched with genuine astonishment at the depth of the Father's love for humanity. She will never lose her sense of wonder at his plan "to reconcile to himself all things" (Colossians 1:20). Although her response in the temple shows that she does not understand fully what is happening in the life of her son, she does not allow her feelings to overshadow the awesome words that come from his mouth. "All who heard him were amazed at his understanding and his answers" (Luke 2:47), and Mary shares this amazement.

As Mother of the Church Mary rejoices in the "greater things" (see John 1:50) we are able to witness and experience through the power of God at work in the church. The real presence of her son now dwells in the "house not made with hands, eternal in the heavens" (2 Corinthians 5:1) and in the church here on earth.

Those who have recourse to the woman who bore him and at whose breasts he nursed, the woman who watched him grow to manhood, the woman who heard the word of God, acted on it and cherished it within her heart, live the truth of this astonishing presence. Those who have recourse to the Mother of the Church are drawn into every scene in which Jesus is about the Father's work of redemption, not simply within the context of their own lives but also within the lives of all God's people.

Mary's son will always "be busy with [his] Father's affairs," as the *Jerusalem Bible* translates this part of Luke 2:49. It is a work that will necessarily draw all those who say yes to the Father into the mystery of redemptive suffering, even as Mary experienced it in the anxiety of this moment. Despite the pain she felt throughout the three days of Jesus' being lost, Mary is able to accept with faith the scene played out before her. In this astonishing moment the responsibility she has for her special child confronts her recognition that her yes to the Father must be conformed to the yes that is the life of her son.

The church sees in this moment something more than the Holy Family's angst over the loss of their unique child. The scene offers insight into Jesus' future ministry. It also shows us another sword piercing Mary's soul (see Luke 2:35). The three days of loss prepare her pure heart for the pain and suffering that will be hers. One day she will hear this beloved son cry out from the cross, "My God, my God, why have you forsaken me?" (Matthew 27:46).

As Mother of the Church, Mary encourages every believer to say yes to the Father's plan. Saying yes opens us not simply to the wonder and astonishment that God has in store for those who love him but also to a communion with him in faith, hope and love beyond human sentiment or religious ideology. As Mother of the Church, Mary invites all believers to stand with her in the presence of her son and learn from him, especially when loss, suffering and confusion seem to eclipse the glory of the Father's plan.

The Mother of God knows where her son is to be found. Every heart that longs to know and experience God's redemptive love should have recourse to the woman whose own faith brought her to this initial moment of suffering, these three days of loss, this anxious and troubling experience. Mary, mother of the only begotten Son of the Father, is also mother of every brother and sister of Christ. She knows where we are too, and she hopes to lead us safely to the church, the temple, the body of her son.

Mary's question in Luke's account intensifies the already astonishing scene in the temple. A child who has been missing for three days, only to be discovered engrossed in conversation with the learned men of Jerusalem, normally would elicit from his parents a more demonstrative expression of emotion than a straightforward request for an explanation. Since it was the Holy Family's custom to go to Jerusalem each year for the Feast of Passover, perhaps familiarity with the city mitigated some of that worry. Yet the hearts of parents are restless when the security and stability of their children are at stake.

Despite the dread and foreboding that assuredly touch Mary's heart, she seems to be composed. There is no hysterical outburst giving voice to fear and frustration. She does not scold Jesus nor even call him by name, which most parents do when expressing displeasure with a child. She respects what unquestionably must have been his decision to remain behind. Mary wants simply to understand the purpose of this decision.

Out of the depths of her love for Jesus, she asks a question that has been asked repeatedly of God: "Why?" She knows that her son's action is more than an expression of adolescent desire for independence. She knows that the nature of Jesus' life is formed and shaped by who he is, the eternal Word spoken by the Father.

Mary is the one person most physically and spiritually intimate with this eternal communication. It is entirely within the nature of such personal intimacy that she can add her voice of supplication. The force of the moment compels her to seek meaning, especially given the age of her son. Is Jesus to begin his ministry already, at the age of twelve?

Mary needs to know whether the hour has come when the light that has dawned upon the Israelites is to be revealed. If this is the time of glory for her son, what must she do? Her concern goes beyond the fact that Jesus chose to remain behind; she needs to know how she is to incorporate his decision into her own willingness to serve the Father. Only Jesus can provide the guidance and clarity Mary needs in order to continue being faithful to the Father's plan. Her question is an echo of the words she spoke to the angel Gabriel, "How can this be?" (Luke 1:34).

Mary's need for assurance shouldn't be surprising. Up to this point she has been guided by angels, the protection of Joseph, her trust in God and faithful adherence to her responsibilities as a mother. Suddenly Jesus has taken decisive action in the Father's unfolding plan. Mary must demonstrate her own willingness to take direction from her son.

This willingness to yield to the boy of twelve betrays a level of confidence in Mary that stands outside the scope of common maternal experience. She demonstrates her total commitment to the Father by her willingness now to follow her son, to become his disciple. Mary will always remain the mother of Jesus, but she will also be his most ardent follower. She is willing and eager to accept whatever Jesus tells her to do, for the maternity by which Jesus took flesh has preserved its pure openness and receptivity.

Mary's question is not an imposition on the decision of Jesus to remain behind; it is a preparation for what that decision will require of her. In the "Father's house," in the intimate communion that exists between Jesus and his heavenly Father, Mary asks her young son what more is required of her.

As Mother of the Church, Mary lives entirely within the eternal loving communion of the Trinity. She is uniquely poised to speak within this communion on behalf of the church. Her life in all its historical richness is not merely a model of faithfulness to God. She lives for the whole church, for all those whom God would gather to himself in Christ.

Mary is especially sensitive to those who long to know what more will be required of them as they seek to obey the Father's plan. She is an advocate for all believers who find themselves challenged by the demands of Christian discipleship and truly want to yield, to surrender and to serve. Her maternity allows each Christian recourse to the Father and the Son through an outpouring of the same Spirit who overshadowed her life.

Having recourse to the Mother of the Church permits the hearts and minds of all believers to be conformed more perfectly to that of her son. In her maternal love she mediates the renewal of grace that allows those who seek her intercession to know the will of God and act on it.

Mary's love for the church, and therefore her perpetual intercession on our behalf, is an extension of her bringing forth Jesus to the world and also of her being a follower of Christ. She holds the unique privilege of being the mother of the Lord not as an exclusionary prerogative but as the unique expression of her personal willingness to follow her son in whatever he tells her to do.

The scene from the temple in Jerusalem highlights a relationship that should mark the way of all believers. The Mother of the Church never loses her willingness to say, "Let it be to me according to your word" (Luke 1:38). She remains an exemplary presence in the church because of her docility of spirit, both to her son and to God the Father. This is the pattern of authentic Christian discipleship. "Blessed...are those who hear the word of God and keep it!" (Luke 11:28).

HERE MARY INDICATES MORE OF THE WAY IN WHICH SHE will perpetually serve the mission of her son. She will express her unyielding commitment to God's plan of salvation through her vocation not only as Mother of God but also as the virgin betrothed to a man named Joseph (see Matthew 1:18). Her espousal to the Holy Spirit—the marriage of humanity and divinity—does not remain hidden and private but takes on human expression in her chaste espousal to Joseph.

The Spirit of God, in generating a bond between Mary and the Trinity, does not alienate Joseph but rather incorporates him into this dynamic communion. The ever-virgin Mother of God has a fitting partner in Joseph, for he allows her to preserve and express the total donation of her humanity to the Father.

Mary's words fix our attention on the necessity and viability of her relationship with Joseph. Part of her vocation is to live within the protective care of the upright man chosen for her by the Father. The Father has blessed the coming together of this man and this woman. He has brought them together to serve the mystery of his redemptive initiative. Their common purpose will reawaken continually their identity as individuals, their identity as parents and their identity together as an incarnate sign of the kingdom, where no one is married or given in marriage (see Luke 20:35).

Mary's words make it clear that Joseph's paternal care is not a matter of mere utility. Joseph is engaged in all that God requires in protecting and providing for the mother of his Son. We can look back to an earlier time when his receptivity to the words of an angel in a dream (see Matthew 1:20–25) reveal his faithfulness to God. He knows that "the testimony of the Lord is sure, / making wise the simple" (Psalm 19:7)

Joseph is truly a father to Jesus in all the ways a child most needs a father. Jesus in turn becomes for Joseph what he already is for Mary: the unimaginable expression of the Father's love. Joseph, for his part, has not been asked to replace the Father but to be the means by which the humanity of Christ can reach its completeness. Joseph is more than a surrogate parent; he is a living icon of the lively personal communion that most perfectly describes the kingdom of God.

Mary's words respect the distinctive place of Joseph in the life of her child. These words invite all believers to open their hearts and minds in appreciation of the man God chose to be her chaste spouse. Mary's consideration of Joseph's unique contribution to the Father's redemptive initiative is also an assurance of her maternal consideration for each of us. We too have our own unique place within the Father's plan to gather all people to him.

Mary highlights in this scene the certainty that the eternal Son truly has become human. Jesus will grow in knowledge of himself through the most primary and fundamental of all human relationships, that with his mother and father.

Jesus is truly engaged with those he came to save. The decision he made to remain behind in the temple impacts the life of his parents. He must explain this decision within the context of his human relationships, because it is through his humanity that the Father's love will be revealed.

Mary and Joseph are not content to stand off to the side as their son embarks upon his divine mission. They cannot leave the boy behind; they have a responsibility to help their adolescent son incorporate the business of the Father into their family life in Nazareth. They have accepted the Father's gift with full and complete obedience. Together they assume their responsibilities toward Jesus with a seriousness of purpose that is the ultimate characteristic of faithfulness and a hallmark for all believers.

The Mother of the Church wants no one to stand on the sidelines, feeling insignificant within the life of the church. She lovingly draws all members of Christ's body into the communion she shares with her son. She respects the distinct character and role of each of us: all are important within the Father's loving plan. Mary's unique vocation is to help every believer be about the Father's business through, with and in the divine and human obedience of her son.

The Mother of the Church truly desires that all members of Christ's body experience their humanity in communion with that of her son. She longs to see all human relationships ordered according to their foundation in Christ. She assures each member that Jesus is the only means by which we have access to the Father.

In her role as Mother of the Church, Mary honors the goodness of what God has created. She calls us to regard our redeemed humanity as a blessing to embrace with thanksgiving. The relationships that define the incarnate life of God's Son are significant for each member of Christ's body. As we submit our own relationships to the redemptive power of Jesus, the Father's redemptive plan finds completion.

CHAPTER TWENTY-THREE
"Have Been Looking for You Anxiously"

LUKE'S RECORDING OF "THREE DAYS" AS THE TIME MARY AND Joseph spent in their search for Jesus is more than an anecdotal detail of this event. It is first an indication of Mary's incorporation into the condition of the human family after its rejection of God in the Garden of Eden. The anxious hours of the search allow Mary an experience of being like us in all things but sin.

Mary knows well that the heart of her people yearns for the Messiah and pines for the fulfillment of the law and prophets. She has observed faithfully God's law throughout her life, with the remnant of his people from whom salvation will dawn. Yet she has never experienced the separation from God that is responsible for the disorders of the human heart and man's infidelity to God and neighbor. She has lived within the condition of man's rejection of God's dominion without being defiled by it.

During the three days spent looking for Jesus, the Father allows Mary to absorb the restlessness of fallen humanity without being corrupted. Mary's yes to the Father was also a yes to the human family. These three days show her solidarity with that family. How freely then can we implore her help in gaining access to God.

The three days also betray the Holy Spirit's presence and power in the heart of the handmaiden of Nazareth. This true daughter of Abraham knows that the Father has determined the destiny of his people; her yes to the archangel reflects this. Now she experiences her own willingness to serve as part of the Father's providential creativity. She knows providence as the "anxious," constant, steadfast action of the Father in the real circumstances of life. She experiences not only the separation of humanity from its origin and its destiny but also God's "restlessness" to overcome this separation. Mary embodies God the Father's attentive searching for humanity lost and on its own, as well as the restlessness of humanity in its desperate attempt to find God.

Mary and Joseph's anxiety in their search for the boy Jesus is an embodiment of that fear that is described as the first stage of wisdom (see Proverbs 9:10). Salvation as lived communion with God is not to be grasped possessively, as one would a philosophical or political ideology. Salvation requires a continual resolve to let go, to surrender to God.

Growth in wisdom is born out of confidence and trust in God, which Mary and Joseph manifest in their relationship with Jesus. They allow him the freedom to be not only their child but God's child as well. This freedom allows the boy of twelve to make his decision to remain behind in the temple. It becomes the context in which his parents demonstrate once more their willingness to follow God's direction.

Mary and Joseph do not fear that they have failed God in their responsibilities as parents. They search for Jesus because of their responsibilities toward their child and also as an expression of their openness to the Father's plan, which already in this moment includes separation and loss. Through the anxious longing of these three days, Mary and Joseph will advance in knowledge of God. They will come to know better how to allow God the opportunity to act within the conditions of real life. Their active, anxious search brings them to a deeper place within the mystery of redemptive love and prepares their hearts for Love's expressive moment on the cross. By providing their son the space and freedom by which he can execute the Father's business, Mary and Joseph enable the Father to further their education in what it means to be subject to him in all things.

As Mother of the Church, Mary imbues the body of Christ with an anxiety for salvation. Her heart shares with the heart of her son a restlessness for humanity that will only be satisfied when all things have become one in him. Mary, within the life of the church, is one who searches for those who are lost, distant or separated from her son and helps move them to seek and find him. The Mother of the Church leads the entire body on its pilgrim journey to "the temple of his body" (John 2:21).

The Mother of the Church is equally the mother of humanity. She shares with her son a universal commitment of loving service, in order to bring to completion God's plan of salvation. She is forever about the Father's business of assisting those who are longing to know him. There is no selfish desire within her heart; as Mother of the Church, she is entirely available to others, anticipating needs and responding to them.

As Mother of the Church, Mary manifests the perfect conditions for our own participation in the Father's business. Her maternal care provides us the opportunity to be immersed within the mystery of redemptive love, especially through suffering. The Mother of the Church, along with Joseph, lives her parental responsibilities on behalf of all brothers and sisters of Jesus. She provides all those who are responsive to her and to Joseph the opportunity to grow "in wisdom and in stature, and in favor with God and man" (Luke 2:52).

CHAPTER TWENTY-FOUR

POWER TO SERVE

THE "ORDERLY ACCOUNT" SAINT LUKE WROTE IS A MEANS FOR us to "know the truth" concerning the coming of God as man (see Luke 1:3, 4). A reflection on the life of Christ necessarily must include the whole range of events preserved and handed on by the church. Certainly Jesus' relationship with the man and woman charged with the responsibility of helping him grow to manhood is a significant part of the record. This man and woman are integral to knowing what it means that "the Word became flesh and dwelt among us" (John 1:14).

The astonishing scene of the boy of twelve discussing holy things with the learned men of Jerusalem is as much about the family life of Jesus as it is about God's physical presence in the historical place of God's dwelling. Saint Luke's description of this event at the temple confirms the words of the apostle John that "the life was made manifest" (1 John 1:2). Mary and Joseph, in their daily life, saw, heard and touched with their own hands what was from the beginning. Their family life is the original place of witness and the foundation for all further testimony concerning the Word of life and the completion of human joy.

Mary's response to the perplexing event in the temple supports the *Catechism*'s assertion that "[her] role in the

Church is inseparable from her union with Christ and flows directly from it" (*CCC*, 964). The ministry of redemption, which is the unique prerogative of Jesus, assumes within its historical expression the lives of all those who obediently accept the Father's will.

All four Gospels make this abundantly clear. Jesus will spend three years preparing his disciples for their part in his ministry. Before his ascension into heaven he will tell them, "Repentance and forgiveness of sins should be preached in [my] name to all nations....You are witnesses of these things" (Luke 24:47–48), and, "Go therefore and make disciples of all nations, baptizing them in the name of the Father and of the Son and of the Holy Spirit, teaching them to observe all that I have commanded you" (Matthew 28:19–20).

Mary serves the divine mandate not only through her unique contribution of virginal purity and responsive and attentive maternity but also through her comprehensive solidarity with all those whom Jesus came to save. For three days she lives the desperate longing born of human separation from God. Her words in the temple–"Son, why have you treated us so? Behold, your father and I have been looking for you anxiously" (Luke 2:48)–constitute not an attempt to restrict the responsibilities of her son but an authentically human response to the redemptive initiative. Already Mary knows that the humanity of her son will enable him to be "the way, and the truth, and the life" of the world (John 14:6). She speaks in the temple on behalf of every aching heart that longs to know that God is truly and concretely with us.

Mary's "business" as mother is inextricably bound with the Father's work of saving the human family. She knows that in order to fulfill the Father's plan, Jesus must be one like us in all things, even in the ways we learn obedience. Thus Jesus "went down with them and came to Nazareth, and was obedient to them" (Luke 2:51).

We can understand better the ministry of redemption within the virginal maternity that resulted in the Word becoming flesh and dwelling among us. Mary's yes to the Father's redemptive initiative enables her to admit and to embrace, within the condition and circumstances of her personal life, the condition of the entire human family. Her title "Mother of the Church" is above all a declaration of her passionate concern for all of creation as it groans in agony awaiting the redemption of the sons of men.

Mary has a rightful place in this event at the temple because she has given flesh and blood to the divine presence. Now as Mother of the Church, she safeguards the truth of the divine presence in space and time. She aches as does no other human person for the union of humanity with God, and her one thought is to assist God in bringing about this communion.

The church is not fundamentally an institution that exists to articulate a moral vision by which human beings can be assured of taking a place at the right hand of God. The church is the fundamental means established by Christ to allow the mystery of God to be experienced as "omnipresent"—meaning everywhere and therefore within the concrete circumstances of each unique human existence. The Mother of the Church reminds all believers that the real presence of God has come into the world, and we can experience this presence in time and space without being reduced, limited or confined by time and space. The universality of the church is the omnipresence of God expressed in a way that accords with our humanity.

The Mother of the Church, through her perpetual virginity, champions not only God's openness to humanity but humanity's openness to and desire for God. Her physical purity is an everlasting statement about the original blessing of being fruitful (see Genesis 1:28) as an effect of being created in the image and likeness of God.

Each person who meets Jesus is unique; the encounter likewise is exceptional and unrepeatable. The Mother of the Church preserves the bold Christian claim that—through our incorporation into the body, blood, soul and divinity of Christ—each believer's humanity becomes the means by which the divine presence continues historically and is experienced uniquely. "The vocation of humanity is to show forth the image of God and to be transformed into the image of the Father's only Son. This vocation takes a personal form since each of us is called to enter into the divine beatitude; it also concerns the human community as a whole" (*CCC*, 1877).

Mary is not the mother of an institution. She is the mother of a man who has been exalted in glory, a man whose physical life came through the power of God, a man whose identity was formed and shaped in a fully human way through the real dynamic experience of family life and love. The glorified flesh of her son has become the means by which other human beings can truly experience and communicate divinity.

Mary's role as mother did not end with the public ministry of Jesus or with his death on Calvary and his exaltation
in glory. Mary is Mother of the Church and of humanity precisely because she is the mother of the Son of God. How well
the anonymous words "Blessed is the womb that bore you,
and the breasts that you sucked" (Luke 11:27) announce the
truth that where Jesus is, there too is his mother. Pope John
Paul II wrote in his encyclical on Mary:

> As the [Second Vatican] Council proclaims: Mary became
> "a mother to us in the order of grace." This motherhood
> in the order of grace flows from her divine motherhood.
> Because she was, by the design of divine Providence, the
> mother who nourished the divine Redeemer, Mary
> became "an associate of unique nobility, and the Lord's
> humble handmaid," who "cooperated by her obedience,
> faith, hope and burning charity in the Savior's work of
> restoring supernatural life to souls." And "this maternity
> of Mary in the order of grace...will last without interrup-
> tion until the eternal fulfillment of all the elect."[1]

Jesus came to save individuals but also the entire family of
man, so that all might be one in him (see John 3:16; 10:16;
17:11). Saint Paul uses the example of marriage to speak of
the great mystery of Christ and his church (see Ephesians
5:21–32). Mary's title as mother of this mystery exalts the
goodness, truth and beauty of human relationships
reordered, redeemed and renewed in Christ.

Jesus came not to eradicate the relational ties by which
we come to know ourselves and experience what it means to
be a man or woman; he came to remove the hardness of

heart by which such relationships are diminished, rejected and demeaned. The church proclaims with the Father the power of the Son to subject all things under his feet, thereby destroying the enmity that would prevent humanity from seeing itself as a "family," as a communion in which we are all mother and father and sister and brother to Jesus and to one another (see Matthew 12:50).

This joining of humanity in Christ originates in the same power that overshadowed Mary's life and enabled her to be joined to the Father through the person of her son. Through baptism we are united with Christ in such a way that we can never ask, "Who is my brother?" The communion that the Holy Spirit establishes is that of a family, one in which Mary is truly our mother and we are truly her children.

PART FOUR
MOTHER OF THE EUCHARIST

On the third day there was a marriage at Cana in Galilee, and the mother of Jesus was there; Jesus also was invited to the marriage, with his disciples. When the wine failed, the mother of Jesus said to him, "They have no wine." And Jesus said to her, "O woman, what have you to do with me? My hour has not yet come." His mother said to the servants, "Do whatever he tells you." (John 2:1–5)

CHAPTER TWENTY-FIVE
NUPTIAL PROMISES

O N THE THIRD DAY THERE WAS A MARRIAGE AT CANA IN Galilee" (John 2:1). This sentence introduces an ordinary human activity, giving little hint of the extraordinary event that will occur precisely because "the mother of Jesus was there." Mary's entire life embodies the communion that the coming together of man and woman symbolizes. It is fitting that her presence at a wedding occasions the opening movement of that business of the Father for which her son has come into the world.

Overshadowed as Mary is by the Holy Spirit, we can assume her ability to see in actual circumstances the rich possibilities of the Father's redemptive initiative. Although she comes to Cana not knowing how the business of the Father will manifest itself, she perhaps perceives that the hour has come. She knows that a wedding is a suitable context in which alienated humanity might be awakened to the real possibility of once again being united with God.

Mary is present to celebrate the life of the man and woman within the parameters not of the old covenant but of the new covenant of grace. For essential to the event is the fact that "Jesus also was invited to the marriage." Mary is in a unique position to know that Jesus has the power to raise up what is fallen and abundantly satisfy the hungry (Luke 1:52–53).

At this wedding in Cana Mary's response to the needs of others opens the gates "that the King of glory may come in" (Psalm 24:7). She helps inaugurate the new covenant by initiating "the first of his signs," which "manifested his glory" and led his disciples to believe in him (see John 2:11). The rest of John's Gospel focuses on the celebration and meaning of what Christ has done and what we are called to do.

At a later banquet Jesus will establish this "new covenant in my blood" with the institution of the Eucharist (see Luke 22:14–20). The flesh that Jesus calls us to eat and the blood he calls us to drink (see John 6) are his own flesh and blood, come to us by way of the faith and submission of Mary. Mary once and for all time provided the means by which all who believe in the Son might have eternal life. There is no Eucharist, no reason for "giving thanks," without her.

Jesus utters the disturbing words of John 6 as they issue from the Holy Spirit, the same divine Person who came upon the handmaiden of Nazareth, enabling the only begotten Son of the Father to be born as a man. Mary secures the powerful words of Jesus in the physical, in that "which we have heard, which we have seen with our eyes, which we have looked upon and touched with our hands" (1 John 1:1). This is the only true foundation of the Eucharist, of our "giving thanks."

Mary is bound inseparably to the Eucharist. "In the Lord woman is not independent of man nor man of woman; for as woman was made from man, so man is now born of woman. And all things are from God" (1 Corinthians 11:11–12). Were it not for the fact of the Incarnation, there could be no Eucharist, no flesh-and-blood presence of Christ within the church today. Pope John Paul II wrote: "The piety of the Christian people has always very rightly sensed a profound link between devotion to the Blessed Virgin and worship of the Eucharist: this is a fact that can be seen in the liturgy of both the West and the East, in the traditions of the Religious Families, in the modern movements of spirituality, including those for youth, and in the pastoral practice of the Marian Shrines. Mary guides the faithful to the Eucharist."[1]

Further, Mary is the one whose own life perfectly fulfills Saint Paul's command to eat and drink the Body and Blood of the Lord worthily (see 1 Corinthians 11:27–29). We can assume that she who said yes to the Incarnation also partook of the Eucharist, as Luke records her presence among the community of believers after Jesus ascended into heaven (see Acts 1:14).

It is entirely fitting, therefore, that the church would celebrate the life of Mary as "Mother of the Eucharist." She remains for all eternity the woman whose flesh fully mingles with the flesh of Jesus. She lives not for herself alone because Christ lives in her (see Galatians 2:20). Her complete giving of self to the Father's plan means that her life and the life of Christ are joined uniquely. Through the commingling of her flesh with Jesus and the purity of her heart, which is beyond human corruption, Mary participates in the dramatic expression of God's self-sacrificing love and becomes one with her son even in his death and entombment.

But it is not maternal emotion that intimately and passionately binds Mary to the life of her son in all its historical richness; it is the communion she has with the Father through the Holy Spirit. "Here are my mother and my brethren!" Jesus exclaimed. "For whoever does the will of my Father in heaven is my brother, and sister, and mother" (Matthew 12:49–50). Surely Mary is paramount among these. This "holy communion" enables her to be an unblemished facet through which we can witness and understand the drama of salvation.

The unity of mother and son transcends the biological tie that binds them because it originates in the providential creativity of the Father. This woman who gave that which is most physically intimate and humanly personal to the Father now communicates to her children that which is most intimate and personal of the Father and the Son. The mother of Jesus is a living word about the Father's love for the world. She was the first to receive "the bread from heaven." It is with humility, gratitude and joy that she shares what she herself has received. The miracle of new wine at a wedding in Cana foreshadows her participation in what Vatican II described as "the source and summit of the Christian life,"[2] the Eucharist.

ALMOST EVERY WEDDING PARTY BEGINS WITH SOME AMOUNT of anxiety. Guests have gathered to celebrate the love between the bridegroom and his bride. The couple and their families want all the guests to know that their presence is welcome. They want every guest to share in the joy of their love. The food, the drink, the music—everything is planned in order to promote this primary intention.

Despite careful and detailed planning, things can and do go wrong. The situation in the second chapter of John's Gospel is all too familiar.

What changes this ordinary event into an astonishing incident is Mary's sensitivity to the needs of others. Her physical virginity is an incarnate sign of her spiritual purity, which enables her to focus on the needs of others, even while participating in the celebration. Mary is not concerned with her own personal comfort or enjoyment. She celebrates the love of the bride and groom by being wholly attentive to them and to their guests.

Mary knows that Jesus and his disciples have been invited, and it is no surprise that she seeks him out at the first sign that something is not right. She sees in this situation an opportunity to reveal the gift the Father has given in Jesus. Here at Cana she longs to share this gift with the couple and with the guests. In the same way that the Father has freely given Jesus to her, Mary understands that she must give Jesus freely to others.

Mary's concern for the couple and her recourse to Jesus originate in the compassionate movement of her chaste heart. Concern for others entails recourse to Jesus; the two can never be separated in Mary. Insofar as she already shares flesh and blood with the eternal Son, it is only natural for her to assume that Jesus too will be moved by the couple's plight.

The "hour" of the Son of Man is not measured by a clock but by Jesus' readiness to lay the truth of his presence in the world before the scrutiny of the masses. What was revealed to the shepherds has been sheltered in Nazareth. Jesus discerns in the entreaty of his mother the same intensity that compelled him to stay behind in the temple when he was twelve. Mary is speaking not merely for herself or the couple but for all humanity. She asks her son to emerge from behind the veil of family life and step into the vulnerable exposure of the larger community.

Her summons stirs within Jesus' heart the same sentiments that will fall as drops of blood during his hour of prayer in the Garden of Gethsemane. It anticipates the consummation of the "good news" that will take place on the hill of Calvary.

Jesus does not fear what Mary asks of him. He has no regard for his own physical well-being or personal comfort; his forty days in the desert make this clear (see Luke 4:1–13). He feeds upon his interior communion with the Father. "My food is to do the will of him who sent me," he will later tell his disciples, "and to accomplish his work" (John 4:34).

So here in Cana Jesus is primarily concerned with doing the will of the Father. Has his hour indeed come? He knows full well that there is more at stake than a wedding celebration. Already he told the devil that "man shall not live by bread alone" (Luke 4:4); similarly, the wine God gives to "gladden the heart of man" (Psalm 104:15) cannot do so completely and perpetually.

Jesus is also concerned for his mother and how his "hour" will affect her life. He knows of the cup from which she will drink, the sword that will pierce her soul (see Luke 2:35). He appreciates what it will cost her if he is to supply what is lacking, here in Cana and also in the marriage of God and humanity.

What initially may seem to be reluctance on the part of Jesus is in truth a gesture of love toward the woman who bore him in her womb and at whose breasts he nursed. It is also a gesture of love for all those who will hear the word of God and act upon it. The boundless compassion of Jesus already agonizes over the suffering and death his martyrs will endure, "because God did not make death, and / he does not delight in the death of the living" (Wisdom 1:13). At the same time he shares with the Father the longing for all "to be saved and to come to the knowledge of the truth" (1 Timothy 2:4).

Mary has a sense of this herself. She takes hold of this moment as an opportunity to speak on behalf of fallen humanity in a way that only she can. She has lived the whole of her life with the weight of her immaculate conception.

While it has preserved her from the stain of original sin and the inclination toward personal sin, it has not preserved her from seeing and feeling the helplessness of others caused by the disorders of sin.

The privileges of her conception have made Mary delicately aware of the human condition. Like other human beings in all things but sin, she can do nothing on her own to save them. The best she can do is to live faithfully the laws of the Lord and try to help others perceive that "the precepts of the LORD are right, rejoicing the heart" (Psalm 19:8).

Mary knows that humanity is incomplete without God. She longs to rouse people from the slumber of their sinfulness. She yearns in the heart of her prayer to give her own flesh and blood, in hopes that humanity could be redeemed and all sins forgiven. And yet she also knows that despite the strength of her prayer and the intensity of her hope, only the Father can save his people from their sinfulness. Like Simeon and Anna before her, Mary longs to see that day (see Luke 2:25–32, 30–38).

The Father created Mary as "fresh wineskins" (Matthew 9:17; Luke 5:38) in order that the hopes for humanity that he shared with her might one day be fulfilled. He made her to hold the new wine that is the blood of the eternal Son. She longs to share that choice wine with others.

The wedding without wine becomes an occasion for Mary to air the yearning that marks the love she has for all men and women. She says to her son, "I know what mankind is lacking. It's you they want! You give them something to drink!" Mary is eager to see mankind drink from the streams that yield springs of eternal life (see John 4:14).

The Mother of the Eucharist reveals herself in the hour of the Son of Man at the wedding in Cana. The title "Mother of the Eucharist" is much more than a statement about Mary's flesh and blood being the same as the flesh and blood of her son. Ultimately it is a statement about salvation, about love as the willingness to sacrifice the entirety of one's life even to the point of shedding one's blood. "Mother of the Eucharist" commemorates Mary's total gift of self to the Father—body, blood, soul and spirit.

Jesus lived his obedience to the Father—a total obedience that would bring him to the moment of the cross—in the presence of this woman whose life was a total thanksgiving to the Father. "Mother of the Eucharist" defines the physical condition of the handmaiden of Nazareth, because it unites her with the suffering and death of her son and places her squarely within the heart of the source for the authentic community of believers.

When Mary tells her son that there is no wine, she is saying to the one who saves that she is ready to take her place with him. She is ready to have the singular prayer of her heart answered and to give whatever is necessary for its fulfillment. Her request transcends the historical moment and opens the way for the curse of Adam to be lifted. She participates in this miracle as she does in the entirety of the Father's plan for redemption. She does not wish to cleave to her son but to make him available to the whole world.

In the simple request at the wedding in Cana, Mary becomes the patroness of the divine liturgy, for the exchange with her son foreshadows the central, unalterable rubrics he will establish on the night before he dies: "This is my body which is given for you. Do this in remembrance of me....This chalice which is poured out for you is the new covenant in my blood" (Luke 22:19, 20). These words and this sacred action are the glory of the Son of Man. In this and every hour the Mother of the Eucharist stands ready to aid us and work for our redemption.

CHAPTER TWENTY-SEVEN
"Do Whatever He Tells You"

THE WISDOM OF THIS WORLD IS FOLLY WITH GOD.... 'THE Lord knows that the thoughts of the wise are futile'" (1 Corinthians 3:20, quoting Psalm 94:11). For thirty-some years Mary has experienced this truth in and through her femininity. Through the power of the Holy Spirit her body has become a shrine to "the breadth and length and height and depth" of God's love (see Ephesians 3:18). The fact of her participation in the Father's plan invigorates her every word, every gesture, every household chore, every conversation.

When Mary said yes to the angel, her life incarnated a truth she had always believed: "with God all things are possible" (Matthew 19:26). Thus Mary does not hear the words of her son, "O woman, what have you to do with me? My hour has not yet come" (John 2:4), as a rejection of her request or as a personal rebuke. There is nothing better than to lay at the feet of Jesus whatever concerns us, whatever challenges us, whatever weighs upon our hearts—including our sorrows, our hopes and our joys. Providence can express itself through the worries of the heart and the conditions of struggling humanity, provided we come to Jesus, even if only for the crumbs that fall from his table (see Mark 7:24–28).

At Cana Mary shows us that faith is not only an act of the mind but also an affair of the heart. Faith is the way in which we live out our response to the God who first loved us. In faith we allow God the freedom to define and determine our present circumstances according to our eternal destiny. Mary has no doubt that whatever Jesus chooses to do will be a gesture of love toward the couple and their guests, while at the same time being ordered toward the advantage of all humanity.

Mary's words to the servants, "Do whatever he tells you," sum up the discourse between God and the human family preserved in the poetry of the Psalms. They are the answer to the question the rich young man will pose to Jesus, "Teacher, what good deed must I do, to have eternal life?" (Matthew 19:16). They are the ultimate expression of the freedom that comes from being a child of God, for they are spoken in utter and complete abandonment and without any emotional, social, economic, political or physical attachment.

The words Mary speaks are "Spirit and life" (John 6:63). They are intoxicating not because of the wine they will occasion but because they derive from Mary's own inebriation in the Spirit, an experience the apostles will know at Pentecost (see Acts 2:13, 15–18).

In the hour of the Son of Man the one thing required is to "do whatever he tells you." We too must speak these words in the face of every trial and difficulty, in moments of heartache and despair, against the ravages of injustice and cruelty. Indeed, they are the standard by which we embrace our life in God. These are the words that allow the creative and redemptive initiative of the Father to manifest itself. These are the words that allow Jesus to reveal "the glory as of the only-begotten Son from the Father" (John 1:14) and set out on the course for which he became man: to lay down his life in love.

Mary's words to the servants trumpet the coming of the Lord, the almighty one. They are the battle cry of Saint Michael and the angels and the celestial hymn of the martyrs and the saints. They express the poverty of spirit that will possess the kingdom of God and the meekness of heart that will inherit the earth (see Matthew 5:3, 5). They acknowledge the triumph of discipleship as a choice to lay down one's life (see Matthew 10:37–39).

Mary's words of surrender set a seal on Christian discipleship, much like the imprint on the hosts that become the Body of the Lord through the power of the Holy Spirit at every Mass on the face of the globe. The Mother of the Eucharist knows that the action of grace is most efficacious in company with a willingness to surrender absolutely to the will of the Father. As a servant of the Father's plan for redeeming humanity, she insists that we embrace all the means her son established, for every time and every place, that we might experience his redemptive presence.

The Mother of the Eucharist is a sentinel of the indefectibility of the church, because she is the first to give her body and blood to the Father with an *amen* that continues to bring life to the world. The fruit of her self-giving, the son she bears in the humility of a stable, is the living sign of the Father's own eternal self-giving love. The Mother of the Eucharist knows that no power in heaven or on earth can separate her from that love (see Romans 8:35–39). She wants us to understand that the loving sacrifice of her son and his fidelity to the Father make this true for all who believe.

At the heart of the Eucharist is this mystery of human abandonment. Worthy reception of the gift of Christ's Body and Blood requires more than moral purity; it requires the purity of heart that is an openness to and desire for whatever Jesus says to do. In order for the grace of the divine presence to transform our lives, we need the bold confidence of Mary. She is the perfect shrine of the eternal life and loving communion for which the Eucharist was instituted.

As Mother of the Eucharist, Mary is not a symbol, a metaphor, an archetype or an allegory. Her life in the communion of the Trinity is as substantial as the bread we eat and the cup we drink. Mary's willingness to do whatever the Father asked enabled the Bread that came down from heaven to become real food and real drink. As Mother of the Eucharist, she continues to verify the substance of this food and drink, which is bone of her bone and flesh of her flesh.

THE SCENE OF THE WEDDING IN CANA ESTABLISHES THE PLACE of the mother of Jesus within the liturgical life of the Christian people, even before the events of Jesus' last days. The words she speaks to Christ and to the attendants attest to her definitive role within the community of believers as they gather together to experience and to receive Christ in the breaking of the bread. Mary's words are simply yet profoundly a summary of the entire gospel.

The Mother of the Eucharist desires our gathering as a community to be an action firmly grounded in the essential truth that Jesus is the Son of God. The community must never be the focal point of the liturgical celebration. Rather, Jesus is the center, the source and the spokesman of the community gathered in prayer. He enables us to worship the Father through, with and in him. The Mother of the Eucharist reminds us that Christianity is not an ideology, nor is Jesus a concept. Her son has flesh and blood; she knows, for she gave them to him.

Mary draws her son into the reality of the situation with the words "They have no wine." These words express the commandment to love God wholly and entirely and to love one's neighbor as oneself. Mary approaches Jesus with the same pure, chaste love that enabled him to be born of her.

She understands that loving God means loving and caring about the needs of others. She lives wholly for others because she lives wholly for God.

In calling his attention to the desperation of the moment, Mary knows that she eventually will lose her son. Her willingness to let him go for the needs of others does not paralyze or diminish her love; instead it enlivens and expands it. Jesus teaches, "Give, and it will be given you; good measure, pressed down, shaken together, running over, will be put into your lap. For the measure you give will be the measure you get back" (Luke 6:38).

As the Mother of the Eucharist, Mary forever intercedes for the church. She does not wait for us to have recourse to her. An intuitive mother such as she knows the needs of her children even when they do not address them to her. Every hope, every prayer, every sorrow, every movement of the mind or heart to God, touches her and resonates within her very being. The community of believers is in communion with her, both as a body and as individuals.

The Mother of the Eucharist reveals for us the true nature of the Communion we receive and the reason why it is holy. The eucharistic bread and wine are the true Body and Blood of her son, true God and true man. They are also a sign of the one body we were created to be, with one another and in God.

The Mother of the Eucharist defines unity insofar as she lives entirely within and for the divine mystery. By freely giving herself to God, the Mother of the Eucharist lives a personal communion with the Father, the Son, the Holy Spirit and therefore with all of reality. Her yes brings forth Christ, who establishes solidarity between God and all men and women. Her yes to the Father's plan makes her the Mother of the Eucharist.

The last words we hear Mary speak tell us that a person of the Eucharist must be willing to do whatever Jesus says. She most perfectly embodies the freedom that comes as a fruit of receiving the Body and Blood of her son. All should approach the Sacrament with purity of heart, with a willingness to accept providence as the Father's creative initiative at work in the concrete situations and circumstances of ordinary life.

"Do whatever he tells you" is the best explanation of the "amen" that should burst from the hearts of all who receive Holy Communion. The Mother of the Eucharist expects those who receive the Body and Blood to live in complete surrender to her son's will. She expects those who gather to find Christ in the breaking of the bread to likewise surrender to the church and all that the church holds to be true and revealed by God. The Mother of the Eucharist allows for no parsing of God's word or the intentions of her son.

"Do whatever he tells you" anticipates the ultimate eucharistic command of Jesus on the night before he died: "Do this in remembrance of me" (Luke 22:19). The Mother of the Eucharist challenges us to hear these words of Christ as he meant them, with the spirit and life he gave them. What Christ has done, we must do.

The memorial is active, it is dynamic, it is real, and it is ongoing. Jesus tells us to deny ourselves; to take up our cross daily; to lay down our lives; to forgive as we have been forgiven; to feed, shelter, clothe, house, visit and care for others.

To live the memorial of Christ is to allow ourselves to be ever more conformed to him, until we can say with Saint Paul, "It is no longer I who live, but Christ who lives in me" (Galatians 2:20).

In order to worthily celebrate the memorial of our redemption, the Mother of the Eucharist invites us to experience the freedom that captivated her life. By her own great *amen* to the Father, the Holy Spirit transformed her chaste virginity into a living tabernacle and her feminine humanity into a living chalice of salvation. The Mother of the Eucharist longs to have us add our voices to hers, to say "amen" not only as a statement of faith but also as an invitation to the Holy Spirit to transform us. And so the memorial of redemption, the great gift of Christ's Body and Blood, will secure our hopes, sanctify our lives, purify our love and embolden our spirits.

The scene from the wedding at Cana foreshadows the proper celebration of the wedding feast of the Lamb (see Revelation 19:9). Mary longs to secure a place there for all of us. She does not compete with the saving work of Jesus but wants us to experience the one who saves in a personal and fully human way.

Mary lives totally for the Bridegroom and his bride, the church. She participates in the divine celebration as guest, as mother of the Groom and as mother of the bride, for she can call each member of the church her child.

Mary is anxious to share the treasures of her knowledge of the Bridegroom. She longs to instill within the heart of each member of the church the same intense desire for salvation that animates her heart and the heart of her son. Her whole being is charged with the grandeur that makes the church "a chosen race, a royal priesthood, a holy nation" (1 Peter 2:9).

EPILOGUE
"Pedagogy of Love"

In his simple yet beautiful apostolic letter *Mane Nobiscum Domine*, Pope John Paul II announced a year dedicated to the gift of the Holy Eucharist. He explained the reasons for dedicating a year to the Body and Blood of Christ by referencing a number of his apostolic writings. Each of these writings is a movement in the great opera he scored for the new millennium of Christianity, a work he began the moment he was elected to the chair of Saint Peter.

The Holy Father promulgated the letter on October 7, 2004, the Feast of the Holy Rosary. He included the distinctive contribution of Mary to the Father's plan of redemption and her consequent distinctive place in the life of the church. For John Paul II Our Lady was a vibrant and brilliant light who illuminates the truth of Christianity as an ongoing event made accessible throughout the ages by the church.

When Pope John Paul II spoke of Mary in the context of this year dedicated to the Eucharist, he reflected upon the importance of the rosary as a devotional prayer that continues to be dear to many members of Christ's body. Within the course of his remarks the Holy Father introduced a beautiful phrase that describes not only this ancient form of prayer but also the woman to whom it is dedicated. "In its flow of repetitions," the pope said, the rosary "represents *a kind of pedagogy of love*, aimed at evoking within our hearts the same love that Mary bore for her Son."[1]

The steady rhythm of the prayers and the movement through the mysteries of Christ's life are in themselves an education in God's love for us. For those who were willing to accompany Jesus, his presence was an instruction in the mystery of divinity and the mystery of being human. The Mother of God, who allowed herself to be instructed by her son, remains for the church the perfect catalyst of evangelization; the whole of her life, from her conception until the physical assumption of her body, is the gospel presented as life. The beautiful phrase the Holy Father used substantiates the titles the church uses for Mary, each of which seeks to entice the imagination and stir hearts with the Love that formed and defined everything she felt, all that she thought and whatever she did.

This "pedagogy of love" begins like Saint John's Gospel: "In the beginning was the Word, and the Word was with God and the Word was God" (John 1:1). The difference is that Mary knows this Word as "son." There is nothing impersonal or abstract about this Word who was with God in the beginning. Mary came to know the Word of God within the fertility of her virginity.

Mary knows this Word who is God through the humility of his humanity, the willingness to be born of her and to be like us in all things but sin. The Word is not complex and hard to grasp. When the Word became flesh, he "emptied himself" (Philippians 2:7). He submitted himself to be shaped by his relationship to the womb that bore him and the breasts that nursed him.

"Mother of God" is therefore the first course in this pedagogy of love. The woman who only knows the Word through his vulnerable humanity also knows the authority by which this Word was spoken. That authority whispered almost imperceptibly to her receptive femininity, and her obedience brought forth life without alteration or corruption of her virginal body. Divinity wedded itself to her, and she knew the Word within the rich possibilities of God's providence. The fruit of the union is authentic human freedom, not merely as a way of life but as *the* Life, Jesus Christ.

The Mother of God continues the dramatic story of God's love for the world and gives its historic events a height and depth and breadth that are possible only through her lens. This seemingly absurd celestial statement indicts the folly of the wise and exonerates the wisdom of the simple. The woman who knows the Word as her own son continues to be an obstacle of faith for those who cannot accept the fact that the Almighty has humbled himself before this woman, allowing her free submission to determine the unfolding of his plan to redeem the human family. The Mother of God allows her life to be a means of revealing the secrets of the human heart, so that where God has raised her, all humanity might likewise be.

The "pedagogy of love" is therefore a course that studies the victory God has won for us. The human condition is such that no amount of effort, ingenuity or aptitude could redeem our situation or establish rightly ordered relationships and a perfect world. The victory that is man's salvation comes only from the God who created all things through this Word that was in the beginning, the God who sustains all things through this same Word. The triumph of this victory occurs at the entrance of this Word into the world, giving it access to that which it holds together in itself.

Our Lady of Victories is the champion of the innovative brilliance of God's willingness to bring forth something completely other than himself: a created order in which he could truly participate. The victory the church celebrates in the person of Mary is God's refusal to allow sin to have the last word. Our Lady of Victories celebrates what God planned from the beginning. She is the gateway through which the Lord of glory enters:

> Lift up your heads, O gates!
>> and be lifted up, O ancient doors!
>> that the King of glory may come in.
> Who is the King of glory?
>> The LORD, strong and mighty,
>> the LORD, mighty in battle!
> Lift up your heads, O gates!
>> and be lifted up, O ancient doors!
>> that the King of glory may come in.
> Who is this King of glory?
>> The LORD of hosts,
>> he is the King of glory! (Psalm 24:7–10)

The woman who is inextricably bound to the Word that saves us, the Word she named, the Word who remains her son, sings the awesome power of God's love. She sings of it as it truly is: a decisive and intentional choice to scatter the proud, to cast down the mighty, to despoil the rich, to show the strength of his arm and the vastness of his mercy (see

Luke 1:46–55). Our Lady of Victories secures the truth of God's saving love as an historical reality. The victory God worked in her becomes the means by which he will secure peace throughout the world.

This peace that Mary's title celebrates comes only through her son. On the night before he died, Jesus told his disciples, "Peace I leave with you; my peace I give to you; not as the world gives do I give to you" (John 14:27). This parting gift is one and the same as the mystery that Jesus celebrates on Holy Thursday. He instituted the memorial of his Body and Blood as the currency of the heavenly kingdom, which is at hand every time the church gathers to do what Jesus has done. The institution of the Eucharist is a gift of peace because it is the flesh and blood of the Son of Man, and he is the Father's gift of peace to the human family wearied in its battle with sin.

The pedagogy of love includes a section on the Mother of the Eucharist precisely because the gift of peace is not a treaty but the man who gave his life on the altar of the cross. Mary knows the peace of God in relation to the hill of Calvary. She knows better than anyone the cost of that self-sacrifice. She stood by, an indefatigable custodian of God's love, even as it manifested itself in the tortured, bleeding humiliation of her son's body.

Mary is Mother of the Eucharist, a witness to the fact that the Body and Blood we receive are as real as the body and blood sacrificed on Calvary. Her position at the foot of the cross is more than a footnote in the drama of salvation. With the church she protects the gift of the Eucharist from being emptied of its sacrificial character.

The Mother of the Eucharist teaches us about the sacred mystery that is the source of Christian life and the pinnacle of human existence. The woman whose entire being has been consumed by the communion that is the Triune Mystery assures us that we can live what we receive, we can celebrate what God has done, and we can worship the Father with the Son in Spirit and in truth. Mary invites us to participate in the gift of peace with the same abandonment that enabled her to conceive Jesus in her womb.

In the pedagogy of love we acknowledge Mary's role in sharing with us God's saving, sacrificial love. The repetition of the Hail Mary forms a litany of praise, mirroring the unending heavenly hymn: "Holy, holy, holy, is the Lord God Almighty, / who was and is and is to come!" (Revelation 4:8).

"Mother of the Church" follows naturally from "Mother of the Eucharist." The personal communion that comes through the gift of his Body and Blood bears the fruit of peace in the gathering of those who have been incorporated into him. Jesus entrusted the gift of his Body and Blood not to an institution but to the men whom he had chosen to assist him. This company of believers is as necessary for the preservation of the gift as is the gift for the preservation of the church.

To make certain that these men and their successors stand united and carry on the work of redemption, Jesus not only sent them the Holy Spirit but also placed them in the care of the woman who nursed him and helped him grow to manhood. In the midst of his suffering on Calvary, Jesus knew that the company of believers would need a perpetual maternity of grace if they were to experience fully the salvation he won for them. He opened the privileged communion he shares with his mother to the real human needs of the church with the words "Woman, behold, your son!" and "Behold, your mother!" (John 19:26, 27). The two are entrusted to one another and expected to have the same unity of wills that forever marks the relationship Jesus shares with Mary.

For the company of men and women united through faith around the person of Jesus, Mary's custodial care is an authentic conduit of grace. Pope Paul VI wrote: "We believe that the Holy Mother of God, the new Eve, Mother of the Church, continues in heaven to exercise her maternal role on behalf of the members of Christ."[2] Without Mary's maternal guidance the church risks becoming an organization without order, a fellowship without authentic human friendship and a marriage without love.

Pope John Paul II gave us inspiration in his decision to entrust himself to Mary's loving care, as expressed in his motto *Totus Tuus,* "All Yours." Those who accept the invitation to entrust their lives to Mary will discover the presence of Jesus in bold, new and exciting ways. They will embrace the church with love and celebrate it with joy. They will awaken to the goodness, truth and beauty of reality. They will experience their humanity as a gift and providence as an ally. They will become like children and be at peace through all the moments of their lives. Those who choose to open their hearts to Mary will be enriched from the treasures of her heart and come to know the Word that is God as intimately and penetratingly as she.

NOTES

Introduction

1. Eucharistic Prayer I, *The Roman Missal* (Chicago: Scepter, 1994), p. 697.

2. John Paul II, Apostolic Letter *Divini Amoris Scientia*, proclaiming Saint Thérèse of the Child Jesus and the Holy Face a Doctor of the Universal Church, October 19, 1997, 10 par. 3.

3. John Clarke, trans., *The Story of a Soul: The Autobiography of Saint Thérèse of Lisieux*, third edition (Washington: ICS, 1996), pp. 65–67.

4. Clarke, p. 66.

5. Clarke, p. 78.

6. Clarke, p. 243.

7. Clarke, p. 218.

8. Clarke, p. 160.

9. Clarke, pp. 174–175.

10. Vatican Council II, *Lumen Gentium*, Dogmatic Constitution on the Church, 61, as quoted in *Catechism of the Catholic Church (CCC)*, 969.

11. Clarke, p. 131.

12. Clarke, pp. 242–243.

13. Clarke, p. 194.

Chapter One: Jesus and His Mother

1. Council of Ephesus, as quoted in *CCC*, 466.

Chapter Seven: God's Triumph

1. From Litany of Our Lady, as quoted in Michael Buckley, *The Catholic Prayer Book* (Cincinnati: Servant, 1986), pp. 249–251.

Chapter Nineteen: Our Means of Salvation

1. Clarke, p. 194.

Chapter Twenty-Four: Power to Serve

1. Pope John Paul II, *Redemptoris Mater*, Encyclical on the Blessed Virgin Mary in the Life of the Pilgrim Church, March 25, 1987, 22, quoting Vatican Council II, *Lumen Gentium*, 61, 62.

Chapter Twenty-Five: Nuptial Promises

1. *Redemptoris Mater*, 44.

2. *Lumen Gentium*, 11.

Epilogue: "Pedagogy of Love"

1. Pope John Paul II, Apostolic Letter *Mane Nobiscum Domine*, "To the Bishops, Clergy and Faithful for the Year of the Eucharist," October 7, 2004, 9.

2. Pope Paul VI, *Credo of the People of God: Solemn Profession of Faith*, June 30, 1968, 15, as quoted in *CCC*, 975.